730

Posh Portals

ELEGANT ENTRANCES

AND

INGRATIATING INGRESSES

TO

Apartments for the Affluent

IN

New York City

BY

ANDREW ALPERN

WITH

PHOTOGRAPHS BY KENNETH GRANT AND
WATERCOLOR DRAWINGS BY SIMON FIELDHOUSE

ABBEVILLE PRESS PUBLISHERS

NEW YORK LONDON

First edition
10 9 8 7 6 5 4 3 2 1

ISBN 978-0-7892-1379-2

Library of Congress Cataloging-in-Publication Data available upon request

For bulk and premium sales and for text adoption procedures, write to Customer Service Manager, Abbeville Press, 655 Third Avenue, New York, NY 10017, or call 1-800-ARTBOOK.

Visit Abbeville Press online at www.abbeville.com.
PRINTED IN TURKEY

CONTENTS

the Buildings

PREFACE

THIS BOOK grew out of a chance comment by Simon Fieldhouse and later a serendipitous sidewalk encounter with Kenneth G. Grant in connection with the development of a prior book, THE DAKOTA: A HISTORY OF THE WORLD'S BEST-KNOWN APARTMENT BUILDING. In documenting the entrance of the building for that book, I realised that other more recent buildings had taken their cue from the Dakota's entrance. Quite recently, an awareness of the importance of the entrance as the critical first impression of a building has been demonstrated by the advertising for new apartment buildings, which increasingly features their entrances. The original list of interesting entrances rapidly expanded as photography excursions revealed unanticipated examples along the way. Gradually, what at first might have been a long magazine article evolved into a full-blown book. Several surprising similarities emerged along the way, which suggested the arrangement of the book. Rather than using a conventional chronological sequence, or a geographical one, the arrangement here is a visual and stylistic one that provides the justification for the transition from each two-page spread to the next. Generally, you will see some visual similarity or relationship between adjacent spreads. The ink-and-watercolor drawings of Simon Fieldhouse capture the character and charm of many of the buildings, especially with his animated additions of characteristic New Yorkers, while the meticulously-crafted photographs of Ken Grant provide archival documentation of the buildings as recorded over several years. The project received enthusiastic encouragement from architectural historian and *New York Times* columnist Christopher Gray, but sadly he did not live to see the completed work. Important additional advice and encouragement came from Ron Denholm in Australia, and most importantly from Michael Garrett in Brooklyn. Additional suggestions came from several sources, all of whose input is acknowledged and appreciated. Shortcomings are mine alone.

Andrew Alpern

Except as noted below, all drawings are by Simon Fieldhouse (www.simonfieldhouse.com), and all photographs are by Kenneth G. Grant (www.newyorkitecture.com).

        page 1, figure 1, Gil Amiaga (www.amiaga.com).
        page 2, figure 2, courtesy Office for Metropolitan History
        page 2, figure 3, Andrew Alpern
        page 3, figure 4, courtesy Office for Metropolitan History
        page 3, figure 5, Irving Underhill B-18768
        page 4, figure 6, Wurts Brothers 112102
        page 4, figure 7, New-York Historical Society, negative 65320
        page 5, figure 8, Irving Underhill C-14693

INTRODUCTION

I N A Dale Carnegie self-improvement course, the mantra is that *first impressions count*. In a newspaper, it is the headline that is of critical importance. And the first sentence of an essay sets the stage for what the writer has to say. The entrance to an apartment house is that important first impression, the opening sentence of the architectural story that sets the mood of the apartment building. A successful apartment house entrance must perform several functions, all of which must be kept in a delicate balance, consistent with the program that the developer has laid out for the architect to fulfill. The entrance is the dividing line between public and private space. It must make clear to the passer-by that he may approach and enter only if he has legitimate business within. [figure 1] Yet that entrance cannot be as forbidding as a fort, nor as evidently guarded as a prison, as it provides entrée to the homes of its residents, who may be the hosts of the approaching visitors. Thus the problem of balance. But the entrance also serves to convey other messages about the visitor and the resident

FIGURE 1. 230 West End Avenue

alike. Is the entrance merely the way into the building, or does it glorify that act of entering? Almost by default, the appearance of the entrance tells the visitor and casual passer-by of the status of the residents within, and something of their collective taste. It is not only clothing that can convey an image of low-key elegance versus demonstrative flamboyance. Is there a smart uniformed doorman standing guard just inside a vestibule, or is the outer door locked, with an intercom the only connection to the apartments within? So many questions and so many alternative possibilities. In New York, entrances are very often approached beneath canvas canopies stretched over lightweight pipe frames. Originally, these canopies were presumed to be solely for protection from rain, and when the rain stopped, they were supposed to be rolled back. On the next page are two such frames with the canvas rolled back just after a rain, in the early 1930s. [figure 2] By the 1940s, however, these awnings were left permanently in place. They vary in details, but most often they are dark green vinyl-impregnated canvas with painted white trim and numbers. [figure 3] Where a more imposing entrance was desired, an iron and glass marquee would be installed [figures 4, 5 and 6]. Occasionally, both an awning and a marquee would be used together. [figure 7]

FIGURE 2. East 79th Street between Lexington and Third avenues

FIGURE 3. 580 Park Avenue

FIGURE 4. 998 Fifth Avenue

FIGURE 5. 344 West 72 Street

FIGURE 6. 135 Central Park West

FIGURE 7. 3 East 77 Street (part of 960 Fifth Avenue)

FIGURE 8. 910 Fifth Avenue (reconstructed as current white-brick building)

FIGURE 9. One Sutton Place South

Where especial grandeur was deemed to be appropriate to the architectural offering, a porte cochère would be created that would allow a carriage or automobile to be driven under cover into a recessed entrance. [figures 8 and 9]

FIGURE 10. 667 Madison Avenue, demolished

FIGURE 11. 125 avenue des Champs Elysées, Paris

FIGURE 12. 51 rue de Miromesnil, Paris

In 1902, architect Christian Francis Rosborg designed an especially grand apartment house whose façade was fully limestone-fronted. To accommodate the carriages and early automobiles of the residents of its expansively grand apartments, he included an entrance porte cochère, which he embellished with a balustraded portico surmounted by sculptured figures. [figure 10] Although they are rare in New York, human figures guarding the doors to an apartment house can readily be found in Paris [figures 11 and 12]. Entrances in that city tend to be more flamboyant and ornamented than those in the United States and are more likely to create a fortress-like impression. Perhaps this is because of France's collective memory of its 18th century revolution. [figures 13 through 16]

FIGURE 13. 14 rue La Fontaine, Paris

FIGURE 14. 2 rue Eugène Manuel, Paris

FIGURE 15. 30 boulevard de Courcelles, Paris

FIGURE 16. 26 rue Gay-Lussac, Paris

[7

FIGURE 17. piazza VI Febbraio 10, Milan

FIGURE 18. viale Tunisia 10, Milan

FIGURE 19. via Luigi Melegari 2, Milan

FIGURE 20. via Monte Napoleone 6, Milan

Italian architects working in Milan tend more towards restrained elegance, regardless of whether they are designing in a strictly modern idiom or in a more transitional one. [figures 17 through 20]

FIGURE 21. apartment house Stockholm

For especially ornamental entrances, we can consider other cities. A particularly whimsical one with much charming carving embellishing an otherwise-classical portal was unexpectedly found in Stockholm adjoining a restaurant occupying the building's ground floor. Here, the stone veneer covering the façade was removed, exposing the rough bare brick, which presumably will be repaired and then re-covered. The original late-19th century doors have been refinished and equipped with modern security devices. [figure 21] The heavily-sculpturized 1884 entrance on Langham Place in London has been demolished, and the comparable one in Prague presumably so, whether by design or as a casualty of war. [figures 22 and 23]

FIGURE 22. Langham Place, London, demolished

FIGURE 23. Prague, Czechia

[9

the Buildings

I · *Dakota* · 1 WEST 72 STREET

Completed in 1884 to designs of architect Henry Janeway Hardenbergh for Edward Clark, Singer Sewing Machine president, the Dakota is the Dowager Queen Mother of all luxury apartment houses in New York. It was the pioneer and set a very high standard. There were earlier apartment houses, but they were all smaller and none gave such prominence to its entrance, or raised the act of entering the building to such a level of importance. The building was not named the Dakota because it was as far from the center of town as the Dakota territory, but rather it was called that by its developer because he liked western names, and also wanted the nearby avenues called Montana, Wyoming, Arizona, and Idaho.

2

Graham Court · 1925 SEVENTH AVENUE

Built in 1901 to a design of architects Charles W. Clinton (1838–1910) and William Hamilton Russell (1854–1907), this was the prototype for the Apthorp of the same architects, erected in 1908 (both for the Astor family). The similar but vastly bigger Belnord was also built in 1908 by a different architect and a different developer. This early version of the hollow-square form that was pioneered by the Dakota is more modest in materials and ornamentation than its later iterations, but it does boast a handsome two-story Palladian entrance passageway with a Guastavino tile-spanned barrel-vault that leads to the fully-designed and landscaped interior court.

3

Apthorp · 2211 BROADWAY

Built as an investment by William Waldorf Astor to designs of architects Clinton & Russell in 1908, this grandly elegant limestone pile with its internal drive-around courtyard was the refinement and expansion of a concept Astor and the same architectural team had first used seven years earlier for Graham Court at 116th Street and Seventh Avenue. The site for this later project was more than twice the size of the earlier one, and it came with an interesting history. When Astor bought the property, it included a rundown building that was originally built in 1759 as the mansion of John Cornelius Van den Heuval, which had become Burnham's Tavern in 1839. Astor picked up on the historical allusions by naming his new apartment building for the mansion that Charles Ward Apthorp built in 1764 twelve blocks north.

4

Belnord · 225 West 86 Street

Fresh from his studies at the École des Beaux Arts in Paris, Philip Hiss (1857–1942) joined with architect E. Hobart Weekes to design the Belnord, which was completed in 1909. Occupying the full block from 86th to 87th streets and from Broadway to Amsterdam Avenue, it was billed as the "world's largest and most complete apartment house." It comprises 175 well-laid-out apartments of six to fourteen rooms served by six elevator lobbies accessed via the courtyard. Comparable to the original design of the Dakota apartment house, the Belnord included a vast subterranean courtyard for delivery trucks, entered from a ramp accessed from 87th Street. In recognition of its distinction and importance, the Belnord received Landmark designation in 1966. This is not the sort of place you would expect a rent strike, but this one pitted embattled tenants against longtime landlady Lillian Seril and lasted from 1978 until she sold the building in 1994. It has since been repaired, restored, and reconstituted as a condominium.

5 1185 Park Avenue

One of only a small number of full-block, drive-in-courtyard buildings in New York, this structure was erected in 1929 by Bricken Construction Company to plans drawn by Schwartz & Gross, a prolific architectural firm that specialized in apartments houses. The large landscaped court leads to six separate elevator lobbies, which in turn give access to twelve stacks of apartments, with some extra-large duplexed penthouses at the top. The building's architectural treatment is superficially neo-Gothic, centered on the triple-arched entrance, but with additional detail on the fully-finished façades within the court.

Ansonia · 2109 Broadway

William Earl Dodge Stokes was born in 1852 and might be considered the Donald Trump of his day. Brash, bullish on New York real estate, and determined to erect blockbuster buildings that would call attention to himself. Constructing speculative rowhouses first, he then changed the game by filing plans for a 17-story, wildly inflated flamboyant French confection that would be an apartment/hotel with the most elegant and up-to-date accommodations possible. Completed in 1904, the Ansonia was reported to have been the largest hotel in the world, with over 2,500 rooms. The ground floor contained a palm garden and an assembly room, plus a large public dining room and a smaller grill room. Rents began at $600 a year and went up to 10 times that amount for a 14-room suite with full hotel services. But those palm days crashed when the stock market did. The elegant amenities disappeared, the carriage entrance was blocked up, and the lounges and lobbies were converted to commercial use. Maintenance was left undone, and decay set in. The rooftop iron towers were removed, the copper ornamentation was sold for scrap, and matters worsened with each new owner. Yet the building was designated in 1972 as an historic landmark, but only after the carriage entrance was uncovered and restored nearly 40 years later was the building brought to the level of what is expected of a landmark.

This luxurious residence of 1907 was designed by William Rouse as an oversized approximation of a Tuscan-style villa, with deeply overhanging tile-roofed cornices supported by decorative wrought iron brackets, much lavish terra-cotta ornamentation, and a pair of massive lookout towers plus a pergola and rooftop promenade with extended views out over the Hudson River and beyond. A succession of owners subdivided its spacious apartments and stripped the building of many of its ornamental features.

Britannia · 527 CATHEDRAL PARKWAY

This is a 1909 design of D. Everett Waid and Arthur E. Willauer that translates a three-story Jacobethan English country house into a nine-story apartment house with delightful grotesqueries close to the sidewalk for the enjoyment of all. While well restored and maintained otherwise, the entrance was decapitated when its over-balcony

was removed and an inappropriate awning and replacement doors installed. But also removed were the planting beds in the forecourt that kept visitors away from the side walls. Along those walls are full-height oriel window bays, which provide special distinction to the building. Without those planting beds and their essential shrubbery, the oriels are floating, and lack important visual stability. A large loss.

9 1107 Fifth Avenue

While there is nothing shabby about the residents' entrance to this building, the truly posh portal of its original construction was the porte cochère and private entrance of one original tenant. That door lead to a small private lobby with a concierge office, and a private elevator that served only that tenant's apartment. Those spaces now house a doctor's office. Architects William Rouse and Lafayette Goldstone in 1925 designed the building on the site of the mansion of Marjorie Merriweather Post (then Mrs. E.F. Hutton), reproducing the rooms of her house within a triplex penthouse at the top of the new apartment building. With 54 rooms, this residence apparently holds the record for the largest apartment ever constructed in New York. It was leased for 15 years at a fixed annual rent of $75,000. Vacant for years after, it was eventually cut into six large apartments.

10 *Clebourne* · 924 West End Avenue

The Clebourne, completed in 1913, is a terra-cotta-embellished Arts and Crafts creation of architect Henry Schiff, here working with the experienced apartment building specialists Schwartz & Gross. Its original marquee-protected entrance on West End Avenue is disused, with the only entrance now through the rare porte cochère on 105th Street. There are only a handful of these early acknowledgements to the importance of the automobile extant, although cast-iron stanchions now prevent cars from driving up to the door.

II

1261 Madison Avenue

Τhis elegant fully-limestone-clad building was finished in 1901, among the earliest luxury apartment houses in Carnegie Hill. It was designed by Buchman & Fox for developer Gilbert Brown and contains its original two 8-room apartments per floor, whose initial annual rentals ranged from $1,600 to $2,200. The building is remarkably well preserved, with the only missing element being the high wrought-iron

protective fence along the avenue façade, although it remains in place along the side street. Even the original entrance lanterns survive. The building makes a significant visual and architectural contribution to the streetscape of the surrounding Carnegie Hill Historic District, which was designated in 1974 and expanded 20 years later. Much of the designated area is covered with rowhouses, but it includes fine apartment houses on Fifth and Park Avenues plus a number of grand former mansions that have been converted for institutional use, and several unusual and elegant churches.

St. Urban · 285 CENTRAL PARK WEST

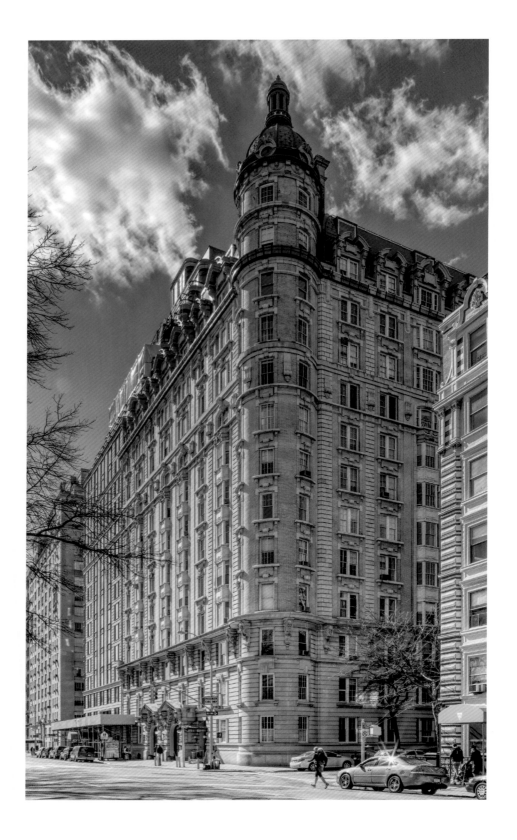

It was not until the elevated railway brought rapid transit to the Upper West Side in 1879 that real estate developers recognized the potential of this immense area. The arrival of the el coincided with the restoration of confidence following the financial panic of 1873 and set the stage for construction of brownstone rowhouses. The opening of the Broadway subway in 1904 had a similar impact on the construction of Upper West Side apartment houses. Developer Peter Banner began construction of 285 Central Park West in 1904 to the Beaux-Arts design of architect Robert T. Lyons. With a traditional limestone base and upper floors in brick trimmed in terra-cotta, plus a mansard roof and a corner turret, the building mimics the fashionable Second Empire French style and includes one of the few porte cochère carriage entrances in the city. The architecture critic Ada Louise Huxtable grew up there and has said of it, "its style and substance were light years away from today's architectural con-game known as the 'luxury' apartment house."

Riverside Mansions was erected in 1909 to designs of architects Thomas Neville and George Bagge. They provided an extra-large porte-cochère, a high mansard roof, and elaborate dormers. The original balconies have been removed, but the rest of the building is in fine shape, including rock-faced rustication at the three-story base and lovely curved stained-glass over the entrance doors.

In 1897, Columbia University moved from 49th Street and Madison Avenue to its new but unfinished campus on Morningside Heights. And in 1904, that campus became readily accessible via the newly opened IRT subway's stop at 116th Street and Broadway. Suddenly, there arose a market for apartments in an area that had none. Charles and Joseph Paterno, who had taken over the family real estate development business when their father died, helped to fill that need by retaining architects Schwartz & Gross to design this large and luxurious building down the hill from the subway station. While the loss of its terra-cotta cornice many years ago has grievously damaged the termination of the façade against the sky, the elegance of the building's triple-arched porte-cochère remains. The original chauffeurs' lounge is no longer there.

In 1924 the Phipps Estates acquired the easterly blockfront of Sutton Place from 56th to 57th streets, and retained Rosario Candela and Cross & Cross to design the first apartment house in the newly-acceptable riverfront enclave. By 1925 the old buildings had been demolished, and in January 1926 the new 13-story apartment house was complete, topped with a pair of octagonal towers surmounting a sprawling penthouse apartment. C-shaped with the court facing the river, the building had three apartments on each floor (the center one a duplex) and originally provided an underground tennis court and a private yacht landing directly on the East River.

16

Two Sutton Place South

In the 1870s Effingham Sutton bought a block of river-front property on what was then Avenue A from 57th to 58th streets, and developed it with 3-story private houses and 4-story blocks of flats — early apartment houses. He had high hopes for the area but was several decades too early, and he went bankrupt. Surrounded by breweries, coal yards, and industrial structures, Sutton's buildings deteriorated into slums. Ironically, despite his financial failure, he was memorialized when Avenue A became Sutton Place. In 1925 Henry Phipps redeveloped some of the area, and in 1931, the last remaining block (held as tennis courts) saw the construction of this building, whose drive-in porte cochère copies the one built across the avenue five years earlier. Designed by Emery Roth, its mix of apartments reflects the constrained economy of the time — from a studio with no bedroom to six rooms.

17

10 Gracie Square

The rarefied riverside we take for granted now as an expensive enclave with water views was grotty and industrial until the late 1920s. Among the newcomers in the vicinity of Carl Schurz Park as the decade drew to a close was this unique building. Architects Van Wart & Wein in association with Pleasants Pennington and Albert W. Lewis visually broke up the 200-foot long brick structure by sheathing the northeast corner section in limestone and crowning it with a jumble of fantasy rooftop elements. The most distinctive feature of the project, however, was at ground level. Next to an exceptionally modest and unassuming single-door entrance for residents and visitors on foot is a guarded and gated entrance to the only block-long fully-enclosed porte-cochère in the city, which extends from Gracie Square south to 83rd Street. Driving in, your limousine can deliver you directly to any of the three small elevator lobbies, and there is space for the car to be parked until you are ready to leave. No other like it.

The Chatsworth was erected in 1904 as two separate buildings with a common ground floor and entrance, designed by John Scharsmith for Alek Kahn and George Johnson Jr. The apartments on the upper floors ranged from a one-bedroom unit (with a maid's room) to one with 15 rooms, 4½ baths, and a laundry. Commanding a fine view of the Hudson, the building offered a broad variety of services and accommodations including a café, a billiard room, a barber shop, a hair-dressing salon, and tailoring services. A sun parlor was provided, which ran across the entire top floor, and electric bus service along 72nd Street to the building. Needless to say, these amenities disappeared over the years. In 1906 an annex was built containing eight apartments, each with 11 rooms. Those, and most of the larger units in the original complex, were subdivided in the 1930s and 40s. More recently, the lost entrance marquee was recreated for a revivified West Side real estate market.

19 *Langham* · 135 Central Park West

The land under the Langham had been held by the heirs of Edward Clark, whose Dakota apartments opposite had been completed in 1884. Twenty years after Clark died, they finally put it up for sale, but subject to a covenant that would keep any structure on the site from being taller than the Dakota. When no buyer was willing to accept this restriction the heirs removed the height limit, and in 1902 the land was sold to Abraham Boehm and Lewis Coon. They retained architects Clinton & Russell to design a luxury apartment house for which plans were filed in 1904, and which was completed in 1906. The apartments were indeed luxurious, as there were only four to each floor, served by two separate circulation cores and four passenger elevators plus four service elevators. Each unit had parlor, library, and dining room, interconnected and disposed around a central foyer. Three or four bedrooms were provided for each unit, along with two servants' rooms and three bathrooms. To make the apartments more attractive for renting, they were decorated in Adam, Elizabethan, Colonial, or "Modern French Renaissance" style, and they were equipped with wall safes, a central vacuum cleaning system, and a pneumatic delivery system for mail. Laundries for each apartment were provided on the roof, and sleeping rooms for men-servants were in the basement as well as storage rooms. The site planning was sensitive and sophisticated. At the rear of the lot, there was a service driveway down to the basement that was accessible from 74th Street. In addition, a carriage could enter a separate driveway from 73rd Street, leading to a gracious arcaded courtyard in the middle of the block, centered on a glazed conservatory (with a fountain), allowing entry to the lobby under cover, directly opposite the grandiose marquee-covered entry from Central Park West.

Befitting what is unquestionably the finest apartment house on Fifth Avenue, number 998 has the grandest entrance marquee of any other in the city. Extending 12 feet out to the curbstone and running 51 feet along the building, this iron-and-glass, classically-ornamented roof shelters a grandiose entry whose bronze doors are protected at night by a pair of full-height cast-iron gates that are recessed into niches during the day. The building was designed by McKim Mead & White and completed in 1912 as the first luxury apartment building on the avenue facing Central Park (the firm also designed an earlier much smaller apartment building at 1036 Fifth Avenue that was razed in 1924). 998 Fifth is based on an Italian Renaissance palazzo scheme, realized in a full limestone façade with a massive terra-cotta cornice, balustraded balconies, and carved limestone details plus decorative marble panels. It houses 17 families in the elegance of duplex and simplex apartments, plus two maisonettes and two full-floor units.

Although bearing more than a passing resemblance to the Prasada ten blocks south of it (it was built the following year), the Kenilworth was designed by a different architect — Townsend, Steinle and Haskell — on a much smaller plot. Each floor had three apartments, and each apartment three bedrooms. The dining rooms are separated from the living rooms by pairs of recessed pocket doors, and there are high ceilings and gracious moldings, yet the planning of the apartment units is contorted, with awkward multiple hallways. Even in an expensively constructed building on an important avenue, in 1908 the level of architectural planning skill was less than ideal. But on the exterior there was included much fine decorative stonework and balustraded balconies, iron railings, and a dry moat all around, with the name of the building proudly cut into the pediment over the grandiose two-story entrance. Remarkably, it is all there, splendidly maintained or invisibly restored. The Kenilworth was converted to cooperative ownership in 1957, one of the earlier of the modern conversions. This has allowed more time for the value of the apartments to appreciate, resulting in more available capital for repairs and maintenance. It has helped that the apartments were never subdivided.

La Rochelle · 57 West 75 Street

This apartment building of 1897 has an entrance porch that encroaches onto the sidewalk to the same extent as do the stoops of the adjoining row houses. Architects Lamb & Rich apparently based their design for that porch on the 1626 water gate to the long-gone York House on the Strand in London. The land at the rear of the mansion reached down to the Thames, where the stone portal served visitors arriving by water. The structure was saved when the water's edge was rebuilt, and can now be seen in the Victoria Embankment Gardens.

J ust as the completion of the Ninth Avenue Elevated Railway in 1879 precipitated construction of blocks of rowhouses on the Upper West Side, the opening of the IRT subway along Broadway in 1904 provided the impetus for a flowering of apartment house development. One result was the completion in 1907 of the Prasada designed by Charles Romeyn for the developer Samuel Haines. The apartment layouts had problems and were modified not long after completion. But the building's operation had problems as well, and in 1919 new owners altered the building, removing its high mansard roofscape. This yielded grandly high-ceilinged spaces on the top floor, but gave the façade a sadly truncated and bare appearance. Those owners had planned to gut the interior and rebuild it, but that wasn't done, and the announced swimming pool, gym, and dining room weren't built. But the original decorative window railings were removed, and the substantial stone balustrades at the fourth floor were taken off.

Built between 1903 and 1904, this was originally the Hotel Lucerne, but reflecting changes in the neighborhood demographics it was later operated as apartments and now exists as a hybrid. It was designed independently by Harry B. Milliken (1872–1952) although he had just formed a partnership with Edgar J. Moeller (1874–1954). Both men had graduated from Columbia University in 1895. Mullikan also studied in Paris and then worked with Daniel Burnham in Chicago and Ernest Flagg in New York.

25 *Graham* · 22 EAST 89 STREET

This was originally an apartment hotel completed in 1893 by the developer/architect Thomas Graham and named after himself. The suites had no kitchens, as a private dining room was provided on the ground floor. In 1899 that facility became a public restaurant, and then in 1928 it was closed, after which the apartments upstairs were altered to provide kitchens. Graham lost his hotel in 1898, after which it was known as the Hotel Brunswick and had a succession of owners. The building in plan was shaped originally like a reversed capital F and contained 31 apartments of two to six rooms plus bathroom. A single elevator was provided. When the individual kitchens were installed and the arrangement of the apartments changed, fire escapes were added. The strangely buttressed two-storied arched entrance is unique in New York and perhaps in the entire world. Its elaborately-carved stonework is well preserved and even the shields flanking the entrance remain although the lanterns they supported are gone. Also missing are the two projecting belt courses that visually subdivided the façade. They were probably removed at the time the fire escapes were installed, as they would have interfered with the essential open stairs. Stucco scars remain to mark their locations. The store at the Madison Avenue corner occupied the space that had been the original dining room. Remarkably, when it was inserted the arched windows along the side street weren't altered, and the rusticated stone piers flanking the storefront were retained. As this was done long before the neighborhood's landmark designation, the survival of those elements is especially to be celebrated.

Built between 1888 and 1890 by Jeweler William Moir as an investment, the Wilbraham was designed by the architect brothers David Jardine (1830–1892) and John Jardine (1838–1920). All three men had been born in Scotland. Moir's business quarters were in a cast-iron-fronted building he commissioned in 1870 at the southwest corner of Sixth Avenue and 23rd Street. That building is extant. The Jardines designed this eight-story (plus penthouse and basement) structure as an apartment hotel for bachelor men. Single men at that time generally had a hard time finding suitable living quarters, as they were looked upon as a lesser breed if they had the means to take a wife but didn't. Sensing an opportunity beginning in the early 1880s, real estate entrepreneurs erected a fair number of apartment hotels for men. As they were considered commercial ventures rather than residences, they were not subject to the same restrictions as apartment houses. They generally provided apartments of one or two bedrooms plus a parlor and bathroom, but no kitchen. Instead, a dining room was provided for the residents. The building and facilities of the Wilbraham were apparently aimed at the upper end of this market. With women taking more jobs during World War I as replacements for the men who were off at war, bachelorettes also needed apartments. By 1929 there were more women than men at the Wilbraham. But by 1934, the building's income couldn't support its mortgage. At that point a new owner began a conversion that installed kitchens, turned the dining room and the penthouse into apartments, and eventually restored financial stability. It remains residential above the ground floor store. And it retains its splendidly-detailed Romanesque architectural design in brick, elaborately-carved brownstone, and cast iron.

Designed by George W. Da Cunha and completed in 1883 as a cooperative apartment house, the Gramercy is the oldest surviving co-op in the city. It originally had three large apartments per floor, each of 7, 9, or 11 rooms, but with only a single bathroom. Under the roof were bachelor and studio apartments plus servants' rooms. Just below that floor a restaurant run by Louis Sherry was installed. He had a reputation for producing lavish dinners and dramatic parties, but nonetheless the venture did not prove a success, and the restaurant closed in less than a year. Steam heating was provided to the apartments, yet fireplaces were constructed in all but the smallest rooms. Lighting was by gas, and water powered the hydraulic Otis elevator, which was converted to electric operation only after 125 years of service.

Designed in 1910 by Emery Roth, the Bancroft Apartments was described by his biographer Steven Ruttenbaum as "a synthesis of Beaux Arts classicism and the Viennese Secession style, with additional suggestions of the Prairie School and California Mission styles. There is no other composition quite like it in New York." Of red brick above a base of limestone, there are highly sculptural copper oriels, deeply overhanging eaves, iron-railed balconies, much decorative brickwork patterning, and classical grandeur around an entrance courtyard. Originally intended to house Columbia University professors and "wealthier students," it included duplex studios, an unusual feature as the apartments were small, only two or three rooms plus kitchenettes. Before becoming Bancroft, it was named for Seth Low, former Columbia president and New York mayor.

This grand Beaux-Arts building of 1905 sits on the site of the large 1850 mansion of James Donaldson. That Fifth Avenue house had been built on an L-shaped lot whose 11th Street portion was 100-feet deep. Donaldson used the back of that portion to build a stable and carriage house, which allowed for a front yard on the side street of sufficient size to permit the assembling of his equipage and the harnessing of the horses. In 1903 William E. Finn bought the Donaldson property. His hope to expand the size of the plot by buying the carriage house to the east of the land he already had was thwarted by its holdout-owner Sophia Tailor, whose house on 12th street backed up to the carriage house that Finn wanted. Making the best of a difficult situation, Finn had architect Henry Andersen plan the existing grand building with two expansive high-ceilinged four-bedroom apartments per floor.

As with so many luxury buildings whose large apartments had become white elephants during the 1930s and had been subdivided, the 1902 Dorilton had been ill-treated over the years, so an infusion of concern, care, and cash by its co-op owners a century later has been welcomed by all who enjoy eccentrically overblown architecture. Yet offbeat but visually distinctive design was not always appreciated. The Dorilton's color scheme "yells Come look at me," according to a contemporary critic who added, "Remark, please, the cherubs, carved with some blunt instrument, that sprawl above the central gate," and "those stone balls on the gate posts, left there for Titans to roll as ten pins." The acerbic magazine critic went on to describe the effect of the structure on the passers-by in language as colorful as the façade itself. He complains that "everything shrieks to drown out everything else," and bemoans the "detestable spirit that reigns throughout," and that "sets the sensitive spectator's teeth on edge." Strong words for a building described in its 1974 landmark report as "one of the finest Beaux-Arts buildings in Manhattan," which would surely bring satisfaction to its original architects, Elisha Harris Janes and Richard L. Leo and developer Hamilton M. Weed.

31 *Manhasset* · 301 West 108 Street and 300 West 109 Street

Finally completed in 1905 at eleven stories by architects Janes & Leo, the building had reached eight stories as designed by architect Joseph Wolf when the original developer went bankrupt. The new builder took advantage of changes in the building laws by redesigning the project and adding extra height. As completed, its south half had three apartments per floor while the northern one had four. Most have since been subdivided, and in 1910 a new owner added the stores along Broadway.

32

Braender · 418 Central Park West

The distinction of the Braender today is its ornamental arched entry and some upper-level window enframements, but originally there was a handsome continuous cornice all around the top and an arch that connected the building's two wings, as well as a series of roofed porch-like pavilions protecting the ninth-floor balconies, which were all supported by spread-winged griffins cast in terra-cotta. There was also a high decorative wrought-iron fence protecting the ground floor, and an elaborate ironwork lantern and arch at the entrance with iron letters spelling out the name of the building. Originally, on the upper floors there were two very large front apartments and two more modest ones in the back. On the lower floors, two apartments were provided within the space of each one of the larger ones. The original total was 46 apartments, but that number was significantly increased when the units were subdivided during the mid-1900s. In the 1980s it was changed from its original rental status, but unlike most such conversions it was structured as a condominium. The condo board has been active in gradually restoring much of the building fabric. The original builder was Philip Braender, whose architect was Frederick C. Browne.

33

Chatillion · 214 RIVERSIDE DRIVE

Architect Emery Roth (1871–1948) came to the United States from Hungary at age 13. He apprenticed within the construction field for several years, working for Richard Morris Hunt, Burnham & Root, and Ogden Codman, among others. He opened his own office in 1895, and in 1898 bought into a partnership that then became Stein, Cohen & Roth, although in reality the two older men had retired and Roth was continuing his solo practice but with a name that he felt might attract more business. Under that multipartner name Roth designed this building, which was completed in 1902 with the large apartments typical of the period. Later, they were subdivided to create small units, fire escapes were installed, and the cornice and rooftop balustrade removed. Still later, a restoration was effected, but during all that time the grandiose double-height entrance has remained, along with much of the fine architectural detail.

Completed in 1902 by architect Ralph Samuel Townsend (1854–1921) for the Charles Lowen Company, this building uses chamfered and rounded corners to take advantage of the views of the Hudson River. Another advantage (allowing enhanced sight-lines) is the 25-foot open space between this building and the adjoining one at number 190 (designed and also built and lived in by Townsend) resulting from an existing right-of-way for a road called Jauncey Lane (for William Jauncey, who had bought the surrounding land in 1799) that once extended from the original Bloomingdale Road (later called Broadway) down to the river. This roadway, running at an angle through the block is evident in the uneven depths of the building lots. Townsend also designed 640 West End Avenue at the easterly end of the block, and 151 Central Park West, as well as many other apartment buildings and row houses. He also was the architect of the Marbridge Building at 34th Street and Sixth Avenue, and the Rogers Peet Building at 41st Street and Fifth Avenue.

This is a very odd building. Its grandiose gated entry is a tunnel leading to a second grand entrance within its inner courtyard. And since its 1984 co-op conversion it has been operated as a three-building apartment house. Annexed to the structure on the north side of 98th Street are two older buildings that back up to it on the south side of 99th Street. Completed in 1904 to designs of H. Alban Reeves (1869–1916), the 98th Street Schuyler Arms was originally an apartment hotel. The architect's scheme of 1901 provided a 20-foot wide side alley to allow windows to be cut into the building's east façade, which originally overlooked the rear gardens of five brownstone rowhouses on West End Avenue. The two 99th Street buildings are the seven-story apartment houses known as the Greystone completed in 1901, designed by architect Martin Van Buren Ferdon (1860–?),and the Rosary of 1902 by the prolific Henri Fouchaux (1856–1910).

The Cherokee Apartments is a complex of four buildings that extends from 77th to 78th streets along Cherokee Place, east of York Avenue. Each of the six-story walk-up buildings was designed as a hollow square a hundred feet on a side under the regulations of the 1901 Tenement House Law. Four open stair-wells in the corners of the courtyard give access to the upper floors and the roof, where there originally were children's play areas and space for hanging out laundry to dry in the open air sunlight. The entire project began when Dr. Henry L. Shively, head of the tuberculosis clinic at the Presbyterian Hospital for 17 years, convinced Mrs. William K. Vanderbilt Sr. to spend $1.5 million to construct appropriate hous-ing. Her newly formed foundation purchased suitable property at East 78th Street and Cherokee Place and hired the prominent and socially concerned architect Henry Atterbury Smith, who followed Dr. Shively's

principles of sanitary living. These included ready access to fresh air, which translated to triple-hung windows that extend all the way to the floor, readily accessible balconies deep enough to allow the residents to bring chairs out and sit there, and stairs designed for easy climbing with benches at each landing. Known variously as the Shively Sanitary Tenements, the Vanderbilt Tenements, and the East River Houses, the complex remained under Vanderbilt ownership and management until 1923, when it was sold to the group that already owned similar model tenements across the street. In 1985 the complex was designated as a Landmark, and the following year it was converted to cooperative ownership.

This unusually-ornamented building was erected in 1908 by Lorenz Weiler and designed by George Frederick Pelham. As Weiler was German, it is not surprising that he named the structure the Hohenzollern after the German empire's ruling family, although there was another building of the same name at Park Avenue and 90th Street (since demolished). With the onset of World War I, all things German were popularly reviled, and the building's name was summarily dropped. Originally, apartments had up to five bedrooms plus library, at annual rentals of $1,000 to $3,400.

SIMON FIELDHOUSE

38 *420 West End Avenue*

This is a design by architects Schwartz & Gross that is remarkably intact and in excellent condition. It includes terra-cotta balconies, a lowered cornice, and elaborate window enframements at the upper two stories. These are all-too-often removed when they fail from water infiltration, freezing, and spalling of the ceramic units. Here, they remain, along with the boldly-modeled two-story terra-cotta entrance pavilion. A more modern survival is the 1950s air-raid sign, but an original marquee has been replaced with the now-more-customary canvas awning. Unlike many other apartment houses on West End Avenue, which replaced initial one-family row houses of the 1880s and 1890s, this one replaced an early 7-story apartment house. Plans for it were filed in 1915 and construction was completed in 1916.

498 West End Avenue

This 12-story apartment building of 1912 replaced six small houses on 84th Street, augmented by vacant land on the avenue. The new building was designed by Thomas Neville and George Bagge, whose practice dated from 1892. The structure they designed is in a Renaissance Revival style that was conventional for its time, but they embellished it with a double-height double-wide entrance enframement and a richly-detailed marquee, which was restored not long ago, at the time when the missing cornice was replaced. West End Avenue was originally thought to be developed as a street of commercial buildings that would service the mansions of Broadway and Riverside Drive that were envisioned. Builders instead erected row houses on West End, which could bring a faster return over the cost of the land. They in turn were replaced by apartment houses.

40 *490 West End Avenue*

Thomas Neville and George Bagge formed their architectural partnership in 1892, when Neville joined the three-year-old practice of Bagge. Together, they produced scores of rowhouses, stores, and loft buildings throughout Manhattan, and especially on the Upper West Side. But their special skill was in designing apartment houses that would provide maximum rentable space within the strictures of the building laws. While certainly not great architecture, their work was competent, and evidently they could work quickly. In those days when all architectural drawings were prepared by hand from scratch, reusing details from prior projects was a practical way to save production time. The faster a building was completed, the sooner it could produce rent for its owner, so speeding the process meant happier clients and repeat business for Neville and Bagge. This is evident with 490 West End Avenue, designed in 1912, and three years later with 325 West End Avenue (on the next page), both for Charion Construction Company. While the buildings are quite different in overall design, their entrances are nearly identical, and the iron-and-glass marquee protecting the entry to 490 is probably what the now-missing marquee at 325 once looked like. At this remove in time, it is impossible to say for certain whether this visual duplication was a result of the architectural firm attempting to compress the time required for drawing production, or whether perhaps it was a means for savings in construction costs. As the owner in both instances was apparently the building contractor as well, this is a more likely explanation.

This building was erected in 1909 by architects William L. Rouse and Lafayette A. Goldstone for developers James T. Lee and Charles R. Fleischmann, who went on to construct 998 Fifth Avenue two years later. Its front curves gently to match the curve of the avenue. There are four large apartments per floor, with each pair served by a passenger elevator. A single service car handles all four units. The building's original 12-foot deep copper cornice is gone, as are the ornamental iron-railinged balconies, but the highly decorative diapered brickwork and elaborate window arches remain at the top.

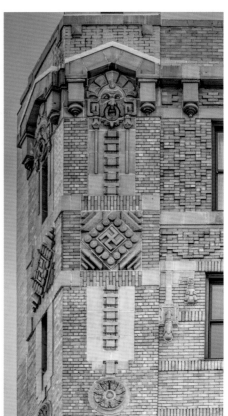

Its Mayan and Aztec-style ornamentation distinguishes this building, as does its northern dimension of a mere nine feet (necessitating the huge fire escape on the south wall). Banker Leslie R. Palmer and his architect Herman Lee Meader in 1916 created a shallow tower of small apartments, all facing west as the back wall was on the lot line. For decoration, they used terra-cotta masonry units embellished with double-headed snakes, mountain lions, the skulls of cows, scowling masklike faces, and various traditional Native American details. Yet the actual entrance was surprisingly simple, so with the ornament widely distributed on the façade, one might call the style of the building's portal "Decoratively Diverse."

The first apartment house designed especially for artists was the 1880 Sherwood Studios at the south-east corner of 57th Street and Sixth Avenue. It lasted until 1960. In 1881, the Rembrandt was built adjoining the future site of Carnegie Hall. Besides being similarly targeted to artists, it added the distinction of being the first cooperative apartment house in New York. It too is long gone. But still remaining as a high-rise combination studio and apartment house for artists (and the artistically inclined) is the Gainsborough Studios. Built in 1908, it was designed by Charles Wyman Buckham (1868–1951), who made a specialty of duplex studio apartments. Also erected in 1908, the supporting steel structure of Buckham's much larger apartment house with double-height artists' studios at 471 Park Avenue remains to support its white brick reconstructed replacement. At the Gainsborough, Buckham placed conventional simplex apartments at the rear on each floor, facing south. These were intended for non-artists, who needed neither the constant northern light, nor extra height for large canvases. The front of the building was reserved for two-story studio living rooms, each overlooked by a sleeping balcony. Residents of those apartments got the good northern light, but they also got spectacular views of Central Park in the bargain. As much to announce that this was a building for artists, as to provide decorative embellishment, Buckham planned a unique façade. Above the entrance is a sculptural frieze executed originally by Isadore Konti, as well as a portrait bust of Thomas Gainsborough in a grandiose enframement above an artist's palette. What is there now are reproductions to replace the deteriorated originals, the result of a long restoration project initiated by the owner/residents, which included replacing the multi-colored Moravian tiles at the top of the building with newly-made ones to match the originals, which had cracked and spalled beyond repair.

45 74 East 79 Street

This unique apartment tower that seemingly floats above a row of brownstone row houses was a solution to the problem of three of those houses that had been gutted by a prior owner just before the neighborhood was designated as an historic district. The solution that architect William J. Conklin devised for Mrs. Florence Gelfund and her two children was to construct the tower set well back from the property line, and then restore the facades of the brownstones and make the space behind them part of the tower. This scheme worked well, allowing the entrance to the tower to occupy the center 20-foot unit of the three façades and to reflect on the front of the tower the sizes and window spacings of the original brownstones, which had been built in 1884 as one-family residences. In 1985 the project was presented for approval by the Landmarks Preservation Commission, but after the OK was given, actual construction took an unusual five years.

Bright white brick and terra-cotta, a pierced parapet wall instead of a cornice, and inventively non-traditional ornamentation were design elements used by George and Edward Blum in creating this distinctive 1913 apartment house. These unconventional brothers brought a radical approach to an otherwise-ordinary building type, emphasizing verticality by careful placement of narrow bathroom windows and ornamental panels to create a pair of "columns" on the avenue façade, whose "capitals" are elaborate terra-cotta balconies. The original iron and glass marquee over the entrance is lost, but ghostly reminders of its former presence are two black iron hooks flanking the second floor windows from which the marquee was supported by wrought-iron rods, and two curiously curved indentations above the entry that reflect the shape of the long-gone protective canopy. Such embellishments were not unusual prior to World War I, but they require constant maintenance so most deteriorated and were removed.

SIMON FIELDHOUSE

This is a demonstration of the difference between a rental and a co-op. Here, the original entrance doors were replaced with inappropriate industrial-grade aluminum ones beneath the original transom windows and frieze, the small iron balconies were removed, the decorative terra-cotta parapet and frieze were replaced with plain brick, and the continuous cornice-like balcony above the tenth floor was trashed. A co-op board would never have been so destructive of the work of the architect-brothers George and Edward Blum, who were unquestionably the most imaginative of designers, producing completely unconventional façades. At least their innovative and highly decorative terra-cotta on the lower two floors remains, along with the entrance enframement and even the original lanterns.

This was the last of the traditional classically-detailed neo-Renaissance apartment houses that the prolific architectural firm Schwartz & Gross designed before they turned their hand to the newer Art Deco style. They filed the plans for it early in 1929, completing the construction in 1930, an inopportune time for renting its large apartments. The massing of the building took advantage of the then-new Multiple Dwelling Law, which allowed the set-back terraces at the upper floors that made the penthouse apartments there so desirable. At that level there are pedimented corner pavilions with ornamentation that is rather Adamesque, plus large classical urns.

49 *440 West End Avenue*

By 1927 when architects Schwartz & Gross filed plans for this building, the initial late 19th-century development of West End Avenue as a street of one-family row houses and small low-rise flats was well on its way to replacement with 12- to 15-story apartment buildings. Two 15-foot wide brownstones were demolished to make room for 440, but the rest of the site was the only remaining original vacant land on the entire avenue south of 94th Street. The pseudo-temple-front colonnade and architrave above the entrance originally surmounted a marquee, which has been replaced by a conventional awning.

This generally-neo-Renaissance-style 15-story brick building has a three-story limestone base with articulated quoins plus vermiculated voussoirs and impost blocks. Two stories below the cornice there is a continuous balcony. The building's special distinction is a pair of elegantly-maned lions flanking the entrance, whose paws hold a pair of lanterns on chains. The address is carved into the lintel along with additional decoration, and on each of the keystones above the second-floor windows there is a series of enigmatic faces cast in terra-cotta to match the limestone. All this was put together by architects Henry Sugarman (1888–1946) and Albert Berger (1879–1940) for construction that was completed in 1926. Placement of the entrance on 84th Street rather than on Central Park West is an unusual feature.

Number 834 was planned originally as a mid-block building with a symmetrical façade, as developer Anthony Campagna had acquired only a 120-foot-wide parcel by buying four existing houses. He had been unable to purchase either the brownstone to the north or the grand mansion immediately to the south on the corner of 64th Street, so he instructed his architect Rosario Candela to design a lavish limestone building on the land he had. That original plan contemplated several upper floors each with a single 16- or 17-room apartment, plus lower floors split to provide 9- and 10-room units. There were also two 12-room duplexes and two duplex maisonettes. The marketing program began, along with actual construction. But then something unusual happened before the structural steelwork had proceeded much past the first few floors. Mrs. Margaret V. Haggin, who had previously refused all offers for her house on the 64th Street corner, suddenly decided to sell. With the acquisition of the Haggin house, Candela quickly expanded his design to encompass the additional area, creating a third maisonette and stacked duplexes above it. The new section was grafted onto the already-constructed original one so skillfully that it is almost impossible to see how it was done. Mrs. Haggin bought a duplex in the new building (possibly the south maisonette, whose street entrance was where her former house entrance had been, and whose street address was the same). She had been the widow of James Ben Ali Haggin who had died about 1913 in his 90s (she was 50 years younger than he). She herself died in 1965, in her mid-90s, leaving an estate of $100 million.

Robert Lenox bought a farm in 1818 for $500. James Lenox began in 1870 to construct a private library at the Fifth Avenue side of what was then left of his ancestor's farm (later that library became part of the New York Public Library and the site was sold to Henry Clay Frick for his mansion). The remainder of the Lenox land from 70th to 71st streets and from Madison to Park avenues was bought by Presbyterian Hospital, which constructed a complex of buildings there between 1868 and 1872. When the hospital decided to relocate, its property was offered for sale, and in 1925 it was bought by architects Eliot Cross and James E.R. Carpenter with real estate developers James T. Lee and Robert E. Dowling. Two years later they

sold it to another investment group, which subdivided the plot and sold the site of 720 Park Avenue to Jesse Isidor Strauss, by then the president of R.H. Macy & Co. Strauss then erected a lavishly expansive cooperative apartment house for himself, other family members, and some of their friends, with the remaining units available for others to buy. Strauss was Jewish, as were many of those friends. In the 1920s, wealthy Jews had a hard time finding suitable apartments, as Jews were routinely excluded from many of the best buildings. When Helena Rubinstein encountered that problem at 625 Park Avenue, she bought the entire building. For Strauss, the solution was to construct one from scratch. His architects were Rosario Candela and the Cross brothers, who produced a structure that was conventionally Renaissance-inspired for the lower 12 floors, and then exuberantly Tudoresque for its upper six stories. For Mr. and Mrs. Strauss they created a very large terraced duplex within which was a separate suite for their son that was cutting-edge Art Deco in design. But the entrance to the building exuded only quiet elegance. As a Jew, for protective cover Strauss knew how to speak softly.

730 Park Avenue

As with the building adjoining to the south, 730 Park Avenue was built in 1929 on a portion of the site of the relocated Presbyterian Hospital, by Northview Investing Corporation as developer. Architects Lafayette A. Goldstone and Francis Burrall Hoffman Jr. designed the building with a neo-Jacobean decorative treatment. The smokestack from the boiler is exceptionally tall and ends in an elaborate corbelled top. Equally elaborate are the floral-paneled parapets and the corner carving of a ram's head. Especially grandiose is the entrance emphasis, in which a broad expanse of carved limestone creates a huge pseudo-portal whose peak extends to the middle of the fifth floor.

Contrary to popular belief, this structure was not built by John D. Rockefeller Jr. It was erected in 1930 to the designs of architects Rosario Candela and Arthur Loomis Harmon by James T. Lee on the site of his own house and the mansion of George Brewster. Both men took apartments in the new building; Rockefeller later rented the Brewster apartment. He didn't own the building until 1952, when he bought it from William Zeckendorf for the purpose of converting it into a cooperative. Once the legal papers were complete, he bought his apartment from the co-op corporation, as did his neighbors. The aggregate price all the residents paid for their apartments in that conversion was $3.8 million.

55 770 Park Avenue

This building was exceptional for its time, as its owner was a woman, Gertrude V. Rushman. She retained Rosario Candela for its design, who produced an exceptionally luxurious product that included an entrance and elevator just for servants separate from the facilities for freight. The façade reflected the duplex plan of the corner units, giving greater height to the entertaining rooms. But its timing was off. Filed in March 1929, it wasn't completed until late 1930, when the Depression had already set in. Although planned as a co-op, many of its apartments were initially rented. The upper portion of the building, vaguely resembling an Italian hill town, resulted from a 1929 law regulating apartments that allowed greater height and terraced setbacks. The earlier building at the left reflects the older law. Not everyone liked the result. One critic called the design "undistinguished" and said "there is a distressing amount of this half-baked architecture in New York, [which] seems to proclaim loudly a lack of the training necessary for fine work."

56 800 Park Avenue

Designed by architect Electus D. Litchfield for Starrett Brothers as real estate developers with an unusually sophisticated palette of classical details, 800 offers a single well-arranged four-bedroom apartment on each floor, except for the top floor, which is laid out in a different configuration and is duplexed to a penthouse on the roof. The building was constructed on the site of an early 7-story apartment house, and aligns remarkably well with 812, adjoining.

820 Park Avenue

Harry Allen Jacobs was the architect of this curiously asymmetrical tower building, but the driving force that erected it came from A.J. Kobler, who had bought the modest mansion on the site and lived in it only a year before deciding to tear it down. In 1925 he had Jacobs design a stack of full-floor duplex apartments to serve as a base for a grandiose triplex apartment for himself and his wife, which included a two-story high living room, lighted by leaded and stained-glass windows and a large multi-armed chandelier. It was dominated by a 16th century stone fireplace and was filled with rare old French Gothic furniture and artworks set beneath a deeply carved and polychromed ceiling. The stone early-Gothic stairway with a wrought-iron railing led to a library on the second level with a small stone oriel window looking down on the living room and its large wall-hung tapestry, said to have been owned by Henry VIII.

Begun in 1913, 850 Park Avenue was designed by William Lawrence Rouse (1881–1963) and Lafayette Anthony Goldstone (1876–1956). These two architects had begun their partnership in 1909 and maintained it until 1926, specializing in apartment houses, although their practice extended to a broad range of building types. The floor plan they devised for this example consisted of four large apartments on two separate sets of elevators within a lot size of 102 by 155 feet. In that pre-World War I year, each of the apartments had provision for three live-in servants, even the unit that offered only two master bedrooms. Expansive entertaining was expected, so the entrance gallery for each apartment was large, the one for the corner unit measuring 12 by 24 feet, adjoining (on the long side) a living room that is 23 by 24 feet. A dozen years later, Rouse & Goldstone went on to design 1107 Fifth Avenue, home to a 54-room apartment, the largest ever constructed.

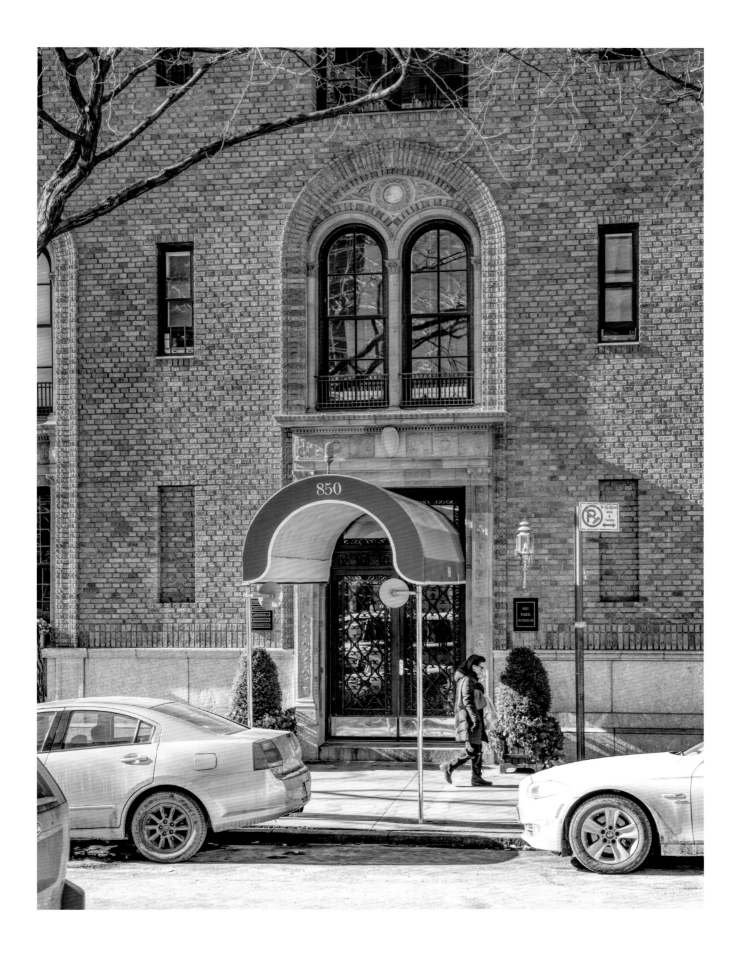

This is an approximation of the Palazzo Strozzi translated into a grand residence for two families per floor. The entrance is one of the most gracious in the city, the front doors being well recessed and gently raised above the sidewalk. It was built in 1908 to designs of architect William E. Mowbray. The dry moat along 64th Street extended across the Madison Avenue frontage until storefronts were created there in 1926, when that avenue changed to lower-floor commercial use.

60 1158 Fifth Avenue

Built in 1924 by architects Kenneth Franzheim and C. Howard Crane for developer Keitt P. Walker, the building is a low-key brick structure with its decorative embellishment confined generally to its unexpected triple-arched entrance façade. Hidden from view, however, is an unusual distinction. While the typical floor houses four apartments of six to nine rooms, the top floor units are duplexed to additional

rooms and landscaped terraces on the roof at the four corners of the building. Penthouse living had not yet become widespread or acceptable, making this hybrid arrangement something of a toe-in-the-water test. Developer Fred F. French had built a penthouse for his family in 1922 atop the apartment house he had constructed at 1140 Fifth Avenue but the duplexes at 1158 were among the earliest terraced units that were available to ordinary folk seeking new homes. Condé Nast expanded the concept at 1040 Park with his grand duplex designed for elaborate parties, with a ballroom on the roof plus glassed-in terraces for his extensive all-weather entertainments.

225 Central Park West was completed in 1926 as an apartment hotel with one- to three-room permanent residences. As designed by Emery Roth for the Bing & Bing development firm, the building included a full-service dining room plus a separate children's dining room and additional rooms for private parties. After 1932, architect Roth lived there with his wife, as he was downsizing after his sons had left home.

This was the first tower Emery Roth designed for the West Side. Completed in 1927, its classical detailing foretold what he would do with the Beresford two years later. The building was designed as a residential hotel without kitchens in the apartments, which permitted it to soar to 30 stories. But despite critical approval of its design, the building was not an immediate financial success. When its operator and those of other hotels allowed stoves with ovens in the units to broaden the market, but in violation of city law, the ensuing court battle ultimately resulted in the 1929 Multiple Dwelling law, under which Roth designed the aesthetically-related San Remo. Originally, there was a marquee over the entrance that was similar to the still-extant one at the Alden at 225 Central Park West. It was supported by tension rods emerging from the mouths of two lion's heads flanking the second-floor window above the entrance. The marquee was removed when the city widened the roadway, with a conventional canvas awning replacing it.

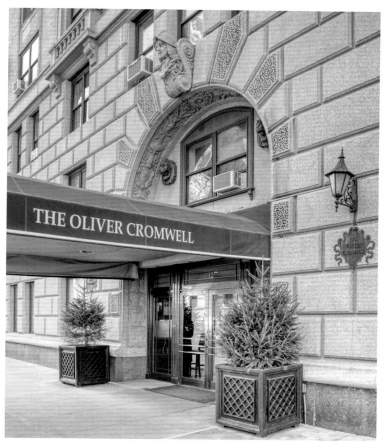

In 1889, the six-story Hotel Beresford was built at 81st Street. Extended north to 82nd Street three years later, it flourished until the market for more luxurious fully-equipped apartments eclipsed the hotel's business model of small units without kitchens. For the replacement Beresford Apartments, HRH Construction Company hired architect Emery Roth to design the new building to the maximum bulk allowable under the then-applicable law. This yielded a huge cube surmounted by setbacks and three corner towers. Its design is lavishly embellished late Italian Renaissance. Just as the once-poor immigrant Jew Roth was shunned by his professional colleagues, wealthy Jews had a hard time finding appropriate homes on the East Side. With the Beresford, Roth provided them with a West Side alternative, and improved his own reputation in the process. Completed a month before the crash of 1929, its finances fell with the Depression but rose again following World War II.

The San Remo, one of Central Park West's grandest apartment houses, was a textbook case of poor timing. Completed a year after the stock market crash in 1929, it barely weathered the cold realities of the Great Depression. Working under the then-new Multiple Dwelling Law, architect Emery Roth designed the 27-story building as the first of the four twin-towers facing the park, a scheme not permitted under the prior law. Its elegance notwithstanding, the building remained one-third vacant a year after it opened. The mortgage was foreclosed by the bank, which in turn collapsed. Then a succession of owners tried to create financial stability, but each went bankrupt. Finally, in 1940 it was sold with another building for $25,000 cash over the existing mortgages. After World War II the luxury apartment market rebounded and the San Remo found a solid footing.

Designed by architect Emery Roth and completed in 1930, the entrance to this building bears comparison with those of the San Remo and the Beresford on the other side of the park. Each is grandiose and well ornamented in limestone in a classical vocabulary with a cartouche and ornamented pilasters supporting an entablature. The bronze doors of 993 are repeated on the San Remo (albeit patinated differently) and were originally used on the Beresford as well.

Before the Eldorado there was the El Dorado, an eight-story turreted apartment hotel built in 1902 by developer John Signell using architects Neville & Bagge. At the time, one didn't need to "assemble" a site as there was so much vacant land on Central Park West that a large plot could simply be bought. When changing living styles called for a replacement, a vastly larger building was provided by Louis Klosk as designed by Margon & Holder with Emery Roth laying out the individual apartment plans.

67 *1225 Park Avenue*

The adage that a man's home is his castle is given reality here. Not only is this entrance formed as a castle with battlements, the detail is repeated at the cornice and atop the water tower. There are also other neo-Tudor Gothic elements. Perhaps this was all to complement the castellated Eighth Regiment armory that was still diagonally across the avenue from the building when it was built in 1926 as designed by George Frederick Pelham.

This building of 1925 connects two architectural firms important in the production of New York apartment houses. The architect of record for 333 was the accomplished Emery Roth, but the elevation drawings bear the initials of Russell M. Boak and the plan sheets show the initials of Hyman Paris. Those two men went on in 1927 to establish their own firm. There, they used for themselves the same sort of eclectic design approach that they used for Roth here. At 333 the motif is an interpretation of Venetian Gothic, especially at some of the windows surrounds at the third and the fourteenth floors, with an openwork frieze of conventional Gothic quatrefoils and a pair of finial-sized lion sentinels at the pavilion-like entrance.

69

40 East 62 Street

40East 62 Street was designed by architect Albert Joseph Bodker and was the final home of architect Henry Janeway Hardenbergh, designer of the Dakota apartments and the Plaza Hotel. Its odd façade can be called neo-Medieval, an unusual choice shared with only a small number of other apartment buildings in New York, including one at 136 Waverly Place and another at 1000 Park Avenue.

70

136 Waverly Place

At 16 stories plus penthouse, and with a large bare lot-line wall, this building is an aggressive high-rise intrusion on its historic Greenwich Village low-rise neighborhood. In mitigation, its design includes some rarely-encountered neo-Medieval elements. The architect Walter S. Schneider completed the building in 1928 for Charles Newmark. Later, working for the Doelger family, Schneider in 1941 effected a creative remodeling of a row of low-rise tenements on First Avenue from 55th to 56th streets that were unprofitable. He re-located their entrances to the back, using the rear of the lots to create an ornamented mews-like alley leading from the side street. On the avenue frontage he created stores. These plus renovated apartments above restored profitability.

This neo-Gothic design was produced by Emery Roth for Leo and Alexander Bing and was completed in 1916. Apparently the last project of the two brothers working together, they may be memorialized in the pair of robed figures flanking the entrance, the one perhaps a warrior and the other a builder or a scholar. An iron and glass marquee was originally planned to protect the entrance, and it may have been installed, but it does not survive. Also missing are long sections of the cornice and its supporting parapet wall, which have been replaced with open railings to provide views for the penthouse residents. However, still in place is nearly all of the decorative terra-cotta ornamentation, which includes delightful owls, squirrels, and grotesques.

72

1067 Fifth Avenue

Completed in 1917, this is the only known apartment house designed by Charles Pierrepoint Henry Gilbert (1861–1952), who is better known for his large mansions. Although he was designing upper-class houses in Brooklyn during the 1880s, C.P.H. Gilbert (not to be confused with architects Cass Gilbert or Bradford Lee Gilbert) is best known for his 1899 Isaac Fletcher house at 2 East 79 Street and his 1908 Felix Warburg house at 1109 Fifth Avenue (both extant). Their style of neo-late-French-Gothic appears here as well, but in a rather stripped-down version.

73

Red House · 350 WEST 85 STREET

Red House was designed by Herbert S. Harde and R. Thomas Short in 1902 and completed in 1904 on previously vacant property that had been owned by Harde. The building is a handsome and unusual design based on French Renaissance precedents, yet this inventively exceptional structure with its distinctive entrance porch was ignored by the architectural critics of the day and was described merely as "a departure from the usual."

Designed by Harde & Short and completed in 1910, Alwyn Court was exceedingly lavish, offering two sprawling apartments per floor at rents of $6,500 to $22,000 per year when decent living could be had at an annual income of $1,000. The building flourished initially, but changing whims of fashion, and more chillingly the changing fortunes of the Depression, put impossible pressures on the building. As leases expired, the apartments were vacated and they then remained unrentable. The last surviving tenant left in 1936, at which point the entire building was gutted and totally rebuilt. New elevators and stairs were built, and six smaller and more rentable apartments were created on each floor. With the cornice removed to allow views, new penthouse units were built on the roof. The entrance was moved, and commercial space was created. In the 1980s a major alteration brought life to the old building again, but 25 years later a third redo was needed to restore a cornice (albeit on a smaller scale) and to renew the architectural elegance of the building.

SIMON FIELDHOUSE

[159

45 East 66 Street

When this building was completed in 1908, its entrance was on the corner, as Madison Avenue was still completely residential. It was moved to the side street only in 1929 when the dry moat and protective wrought-iron railings were removed and stores created along the avenue. Architects Herbert Harde and Richard Thomas Short looked to 15th and 16th century Flemish Gothic architecture for design inspiration here. The confection they produced also includes French and Elizabethan English motifs, and serves as a paean to the decorative possibilities of terra-cotta.

The entrance and lobby of 44 West 77 Street are surely the most flamboyantly Gothic of any in New York. But originally the building overall was even more so. There were lacy arches over many of the windows, and the ornamentation at the upper floors and roof line appeared to have been squeezed out of a cake-baker's pastry-frosting tube. But nearly all of that terra-cotta embellishment had been defective when installed in 1909, and was reattached two years later. Sadly, by 1945 it had deteriorated so much further that is was removed, except at the lower floors and at a chimney flanking the tower roof. The architects for the building were Richard Thomas Short, born about 1870, and his partner Herbert Spencer Steinhardt (who was born about 1873 and later changed his name to Herbert Harde). They had a long career designing high-rise apartment houses, the four that are included here undoubtedly being the most distinctive eye-catchers ever produced by any architects in New York.

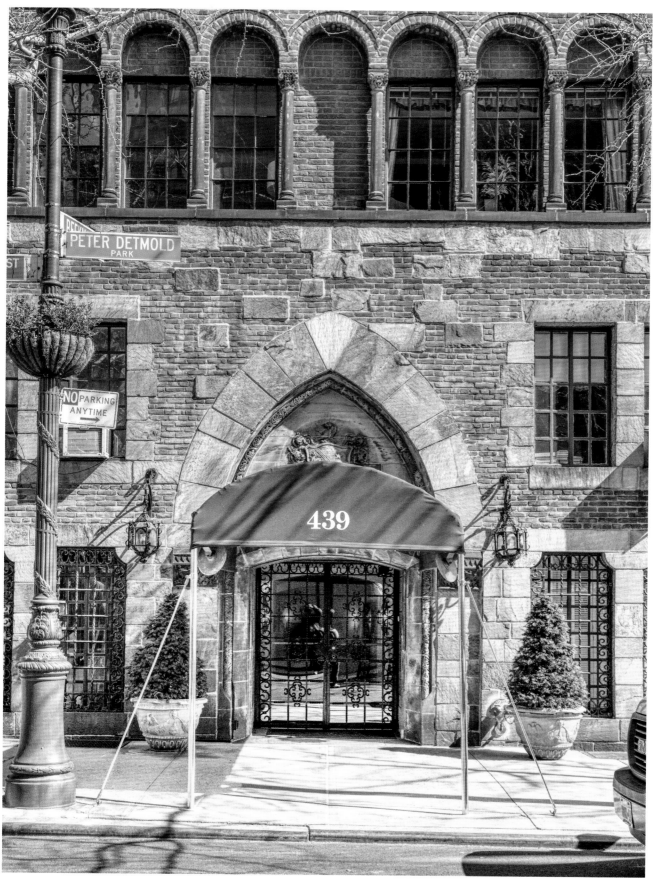

See overleaf for the text concerning this building.

It is quite rare to find a pair of apartment buildings that are such close siblings on their façades as 145 West 79 Street (upper photo opposite) and 439 East 51 Street (lower photo and previous spread). The primary architects for both were Van Wart & Wein with Treanor & Fatio consulting to them. Completion of the two buildings was in 1925. The west side venture was named Manchester House and the east side one was called Beekman Mansion, with the name painted in large bold letters at the top of the west-facing lot-line wall. Both buildings have pseudo-heraldic shields over the entrances. The 79th Street building is smaller, with modest apartments above two doctors' offices flanking the entrance. The other building includes more expansive apartments and duplex maisonettes in place of the offices. The 51st Street front is embellished with relief carvings in the stone lintels over some of the ground-floor openings. They depict a hunter on horseback with his hounds and blowing his horn; Neptune traditionally shown; a scholar reading by lamplight; and a trio of medieval singers holding a long scroll. All quite exceptional and inexplicable.

79 *Campanile* · 450 East 52 Street

In 1920, Sutton Place was created as an enclave of upper-class residences. This was a replacement for the existing tenement and row house development of Effingham B. Sutton from the 1870s that had proved an economic failure and had deteriorated into a slum. Those decrepit buildings and the many industrial uses that had accumulated along the East River made the area ripe for redevelopment. The pioneer was a block of private houses surrounding a communal lawn, followed by several luxurious high-rise apartment houses. The driving force was a group of aggressive, accomplished, wealthy women that included Anne Morgan, Mrs. William K. Vanderbilt, Elsie de Wolfe, and Elizabeth Marbury. South of Sutton Place but unconnected to it is Beekman Place. At its north end, Joseph G. Thomas in 1924 developed the Venetian-styled Beekman Terrace at 455 East 51 Street, designed by James E.R. Carpenter with the assistance of Treanor & Fatio. Two years later, that firm joined with Van Wart & Wein to design Beekman Mansion immediately to the west at 439 East 51 Street, also for Thomas. With first a six-story and then a ten-story apartment building under his belt, Thomas then embarked on a high-rise project beginning in 1926. Van Wart & Wein was the sole architect that Joseph Thomas used for the Campanile, a soaring nominally-Gothic slab that originally offered waterfront garden apartments below the street level and a private boat landing at the water's edge. The intrusion of the East River Drive destroyed those amenities, but the three levels below the street nonetheless retained their open river views just barely over the roofs of the passing automobiles.

This is a distinctive and unusual contributor to the Central Park West streetscape on two counts. At six stories, it is a low-rise building in a high-rise neighborhood. And its neo-Tudor half-timbered and gabled style is rare in Manhattan. The special distinction here are the sixth floor apartments, which have extra-height angled ceilings under the sloping roofs plus wood-burning fireplaces. The building was designed and constructed by the Fred F. French Company in 1918, under a financial plan that allowed small investors to participate. The French company thrived under this arrangement and went on to build Tudor City in the East 40s. Mr. French was a pioneer in penthouse living, successively constructing ones for his family atop two Fifth Avenue apartment buildings he constructed at 1140 and then 1010.

81

243 West End Avenue

This 1925 project of Emery Roth was originally an apartment-hotel called The Cardinal, and shows how architects gain inspiration from other architects, or perhaps from aggressive salesmen of specialty materials. A visually distinctive feature at the third floor above the entrance here is an elaborate polychrome terra-cotta arcade of Spanish Colonial Revival design. Curiously, an identical (but shorter) arcade appears in the same position above the entrance to 52 Riverside Drive, designed about the same time by architects Deutsch & Schneider and also at 147 West 79 Street by Jacob M. Felson. Conceptually similar to the arcades on these three buildings (and even more so to each other) are the polychrome terra-cotta round-arched arcades above the entrances to 39 Fifth Avenue, designed in 1922 by Emery Roth, and to 37 Washington Square West, completed in 1928 to the design of architects Gronenberg & Leuchtag. Photographs and descriptions follow for these buildings whose façade aesthetics are so related.

82

147 West 79 Street

Jacob M. Felson designed this building in 1925 at the same time Emery Roth designed 243 West End Avenue. The polychrome terra-cotta third-floor arcades and paired window surrounds on both buildings are identical. The pace of residential construction in the middle of the 1920s put a premium on time saving both in the production of working drawings and the completion of projects. Ergo, standard materials.

83

52 Riverside Drive

This is one of a trio of curiously similar buildings. Drawings for this one were filed in 1925 by Maurice Deutsch (1884–1957) and Walter Schneider (1890–?). It includes at the third and thirteenth floors identical four-window ornamental arcades of polychrome terra-cotta. Identical arcades are found on 147 West 79 Street (Jacob M. Felson), and longer ones appear on 243 West End Avenue (Emery Roth). The entrance enframement on the 79th Street building is nearly identical to this one. As architects by nature are creative and individualistic, it is curious why three of them, at the same time, would put on these three buildings the same highly distinctive, brightly colored design elements, especially as the three are within the same neighborhood only a few blocks of each other. A puzzlement indeed.

84 *39 Fifth Avenue*

This was one of the earliest high-rise residences built on lower Fifth Avenue, contributing to the rapid redevelopment of Greenwich Village following the first World War. Emery Roth designed this fourteen-story and penthouse building for the Bing & Bing building firm in 1922. It was constructed on the site of a grand 54-foot-wide Anglo-Italianate mansion of the 1850s and adjoining another one, which itself was replaced a year later by another tall apartment house designed by Rosario Candela. Roth embellished the façade with an arcade and balconette in polychrome glazed terra-cotta in a neo-Spanish Renaissance style. In a curious bit of architectural imitation, this ornamentation was copied five years later at the apartment house at 37 Washington Square West by architects Herman Gronenberg (1889–1931) and Albert J.H. Leuchtag (d.1959).

Completed about five years after Emery Roth's 39 Fifth Avenue, this building by Gronenberg & Leuchtag appears to have taken the earlier effort's polychrome terracotta design scheme and modified it only in minute details. Even the pinwheel medallions on the balconies are near-duplicates. At that time, the concept of copyright protection for architectural designs didn't exist. Even the construction drawings could be copied. But the entrances to the two buildings are completely different.

Millan House · 116 East 68 Street

This is one of a pair of midblock build-ings at 67th and 68th Streets separat-ed by a landscaped garden, all designed by Andrew J. Thomas and built in 1931 by John D. Rockefeller Jr. The buildings are neo-Romanesque with dark brick over a base of butterscotch-brown stone that has been carved with a profusion of fearsome owls and bulldogs, plus ready-to-pounce dogs, cats, and malevolent rabbits. Unusual ornament is not hard to find on New York apartment houses but such an extensive menagerie as this is surely unique, especially when as well integrated in a pair of buildings that are so well maintained.

SIMON FIELDHOUSE

London Terrace was begun just before the 1929 financial crash by Henry Mandel, whose bold financial moves and brash personality may have been the model for Harry Macklowe of our time. The four corner buildings were constructed in 1931, a year after the smaller mid-block structures had been completed. The entire complex is fully interconnected at the ground floor and the basement, easing residents' access to the on-site shops and services. As an outgrowth of a 1934 foreclosure, the corner buildings are now co-ops, while all the lower buildings are rentals under a single ownership. The 1,685 apartments were originally intended as affordable housing for working people, with monthly rents at the beginning averaging $30 per room. Yet included was a large swimming pool and a recreational roof deck fitted out to resemble an ocean liner. The architects were Victor Farrar and Richard Watmaugh.

In 1924, Arthur Brisbane bought the northeast corner of Fifth Avenue and 102nd Street. He was a columnist for the Hearst newspapers and was then in the process of developing the Ritz Tower at 57th and Park Avenue. It was predicted that he would build a garage on the site, but instead in 1928 he hired Schultz & Weaver to design an apartment house there. The building that resulted was unusual in two respects. At a time when classical styles were customary for upper-class residences, this one was Romanesque, verging on the Medieval, with a caramel-colored brick above a limestone base and with limestone ornamentation at the top. But what was really special about 1215 was only minimally evident on the façade. The 14th, 15th, and penthouse floors of the building comprised a grandiose apartment for Brisbane himself. This expansive triplex was centered on a baronial 2-storied living room 60 feet long with a fireplace at each end. Adjoining was a 33-foot dining hall (also with a double-height ceiling) plus a study *and* a library. The master suite shared the floor with the more public rooms, while one flight above were six spacious guest rooms, each with its own bath. There was a greenhouse at the roof level, with the apartment served by a private elevator and its own open stair hall. After Brisbane died in 1936 and the building's mortgage was foreclosed in 1939, his apartment was subdivided into several smaller units.

This Romanesque Revival-style apartment house with its pair of curiously human-faced guardian lions holding heraldic shields was built in 1924 to a design of Rosario Candela. It replaced three brownstone row houses, but evidently the corner house of 1892 (Clarence True, architect) was a holdout and declined to sell. That house was designated an individual landmark in 1988. With its unusual curved corner and small upper-floor terrace it enhances the neighborhood and provides southern views from what would otherwise be a blank lot-line wall.

522

90

30 East 76 Street

Although much better known for the Empire State Building, Shreve, Lamb & Harmon produced architecture in a wide variety of styles. Here in 1929 they used a Venetian Renaissance vocabulary, with a highly textured brick of considerable visual interest. They used the brick in ways that more conventionally would have employed stone or terra-cotta. What results is a building with a warmly inviting feel appropriate to its original use as an apartment house, but fortuitously also suited to its later incarnation as medical offices and a small hospital.

91

898 Park Avenue

Early in 1924, Henry Mandel was riding high on a series of successful real estate ventures, and had just completed the block-long Pershing Square Building on Park Avenue from 41st to 42nd Streets. His architects, John Sloan and Albert E. Nast, had distinguished their design for that building by using northern Italian pre-Renaissance design elements, giving an inviting appeal to the structure. As these Tuscan motifs were successful, Mandel decided to use them for a new apartment house project he was planning two miles north at 79th Street, albeit on a domestic scale. Retaining the same architectural team, Mandel had them plan a rectangular tower without setbacks on the 75- by 41-foot site, comprising six stacked duplex apartments plus a single-floor unit on the second floor and a doctor's suite at the ground level. The duplex suites were more than 5,000 square feet apiece, but were compactly planned and had the feel of a private house. The building was a co-op, with the 13-room duplexes selling for $54,000 to $62,000 with monthly maintenance charges averaging $700.

Each of the building's four elevator men earned $20 a week, and the total annual labor cost, all-inclusive for the nine service people at the building was less than $10,000. That was 1924. Then came the Great Depression and with it the foreclosures that doomed so many of the grand old apartments of the earlier, more prosperous years. Only two of the original duplexes of 898 Park Avenue have survived, the rest having been converted in 1948 by architect Simon Zelnick to simplex units — still large, but nowhere near as grand as what had originally been built. And the gracious curving staircases were destroyed in the process. But a triplex was created more recently at the top of the building, with a terrace at the penthouse level, and an expansive master suite at the very top of the building. Despite all these changes, 898 remains as a simple rectangular block set off on each side by a low-rise brownstone rowhouse, adding to the visual distinction of this Tuscan Tapestry Tower.

92 *444 Central Park West*

At 104th Street, far north of comparable buildings, the 174-foot tall 444 towers over its older neighbors. Completed in 1930 for developer William Hanna, it was designed by Russell M. Boak and Hyman Paris, who had met when they both worked for Emery Roth. This Tuscan Romanesque design used a richly variegated palette of brick, including rough-cut blackened clinker brick, combining it with tawny-colored cast stone and terra-cotta of a similar hue. The Multiple Dwelling Law of 1929 under which it was built allowed a series of penthouse setbacks at the top, culminating in a decorated enclosure for the essential wooden water tank. The verticality of the design continued down past a quartet of charming pelicans to an arcade over the canopied entrance.

93 *Gramont* · 215 West 98 Street

This is an uncharacteristically conventional classically-detailed building designed by brothers George and Edward Blum. Completed in 1911, it is elegantly executed and has been splendidly restored. Its most imaginative and unconventional feature is its entrance, recessed and unnoticed behind a deep courtyard.

A 1928 high-rise amidst an established 19th century low-rise historic district, the Remsen provides studio and one-bedroom apartments in a neighborhood of 20-room private houses that was designated in 1965 by the Landmarks Preservation Commission as its first Historic District. It was designed by Hyman Isaac Feldman (1896–1981) for developer Simon Silk in a Tuscan Romanesque style that includes whimsical stone carvings, at least one of which probably represents someone connected with the project. Feldman was a Ukrainian immigrant with a broad architectural practice, better known for his later Art Deco designs.

95 *47 Plaza Street* · BROOKLYN

Park Slope, Brooklyn, was developed late in the 19th century with row houses on the side streets and more expansive mansions facing Prospect Park. One such house was erected on a spacious but restrictive triangular lot at the southwest corner of Grand Army Plaza, pictured here about 1890. Four decades later, in 1928, a replacement was completed. Architect Rosario Candela was a skilled designer much in demand in Manhattan, but this was only the second apartment house he had built in Brooklyn. From the right angle, it looks like a stage set.

Imperial · 1198 Pacific Street, Brooklyn
Renaissance · 488 Nostrand Avenue, Brooklyn

The Renaissance (above) and the Imperial (right and left) were built by developer Louis F. Seitz in 1892 to drawings prepared by Montrose W. Morris (1861–1916). Two years earlier Seitz had employed Morris to design the much larger Alhambra apartment house on Nostrand Avenue, which was well received and presumably was the impetus for the these two smaller projects. All three buildings offered large apartments to a generally upper middle-class tenancy, until the economy and the neighborhood deteriorated in the 1970s. Abandoned to unpaid taxes, they were eventually taken by the city and then gut-renovated and returned to viability.

This 8-story early apartment house of 1910 doubtless was viewed when new as being over-bearingly tall and aesthetically out of place for its decidedly low-rise historic neighborhood of Brooklyn Heights. It was designed by William Alcephron Boring (1859–1937), an architect who pioneered off-the-foyer plan layouts and functional separation in apartments even before Messrs Candela, Carpenter, and Roth perfected them. With his partner Edward L. Tilton he designed the Ellis Island Immigration Station in 1900 in addition to apartment buildings and many private residences. Boring retired five years after this building was finished.

The curious name of Tennis Court dates to 1886 when entrepreneur Richard Flicken planned a development that would create a consistent enclave. He laid out streets, installed utilities, surveyed 50-foot wide lots and imposed design restrictions, resulting in a group of large villas fronted with lush lawns. By the 1920s, such housing no longer met the needs of the neighborhood, so in short order the houses were collectively replaced with large apartment buildings. One of the grandest was a complex with the preposterous name of Chateau Frontenac. Designed by William T. McCarthy, it has a triple-arched entrance in the manner of the French Renaissance of François I, with groin-vaulted entries and a landscaped interior courtyard. But the tenantry of the flush 1920s exited and the project deteriorated. An enlightened corporate owner has been restoring its faded elegance, but this has necessitated elaborate security fencing and gates. Surprisingly, this has been accomplished with sensitivity, taste, and a measure of flair.

Designed by architect Martyn N. Weinstein and completed in 1935, this six-story semi-fire-proof building is representative of the large number of apartment houses erected during the 1930s in the outer boroughs that employ Art Deco motifs as a means of distinguishing their façades. This is accomplished here at minimal cost by careful use of two colors of brick in stripes and a zig-zag frieze at the ground floor plus decorative colored terra-cotta panels between the windows and at the para-pet wall. The most vivid terra-cotta is reserved for the entrance, where it is both glazed and colored. The black and gold color scheme at the entrance coincidentally is favored by the neighborhood's now largely Russian residents.

336 Central Park West

One of only three Art Deco buildings on Central Park West that were designed by the prolific apartment house specialists Simon I. Schwartz (1877–1956) and Arthur Gross (1877–1950), number 336 is an exceptional design within the entire city, as it has a distinctly Egyptian feel at the top, with a plum-colored lotus-form terra-cotta cornice and matching ornamentation of the rooftop structure enclosing the wooden water tower. The façade is a subtle and quietly elegant composition with unusual brickwork patterns and colors.

55 Central Park West

Schwartz & Gross were journeymen apartment house architects skilled in producing buildings in the standard historicist styles favored by conservative developers, which they had done since the early 1900s. But following a low-key but decidedly different design for 336 Central Park West in 1928, the next year they produced this full-blown Art Deco building, the first of a group that defines Central Park West as the Art Deco "capital" in the city. Two elements stand out: the spiky ziggurat-like buttresses and finials at the lower floors and at the upper set-back floors, and the shaded coloring of the brickwork, running from deep purple at the second floor, gradually lightening to a pale yellowish white at the top. Even the entrance marquee carries through the ziggurat theme. Within the units, most living rooms are dropped a few steps below the other rooms in the apartment to give them greater importance.

Architects Simon Schwartz and Arthur Gross formed a partnership in 1902, specializing in apartment houses, of which they produced a very large number. Adept at working in a variety of styles, and apparently to any budget, they utilized the Beaux-Arts and neo-Renaissance styles in the early 1900s, switching to Georgian, Colonial, and neo-Gothic as tastes shifted. When the Art Deco style became chic, in 1928 they molded it into a lotus-flower theme at the roof level of 336 Central Park West, giving the building a neo-Egyptian flavor, following it in 1929 with the distinctive terra-cotta embellished façade of 55 Central Park West. The following year, for the same developer they designed 241 Central Park West, employing plant-like forms at the base executed in golden-yellow terra-cotta, and similar lotus-like ornament at the upper section. The elaborately Art Deco marquee at the entrance to 55 Central Park West has been restored, but the identical one at 241 Central Park West no longer exists and was replaced with a conventional canvas canopy. The two rowhouses from 1888 shown adjoining 241 in the photograph were originally part of a row of nine.

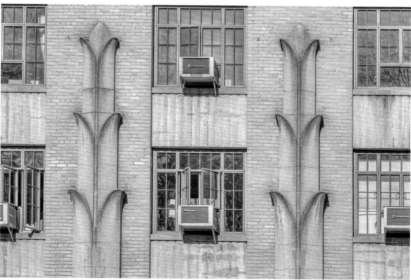

Developer Irwin Chanin and architect Jacques Delemarre designed the 1931 occupancy of this building for a market that had been hard hit by the Depression. No longer able to afford the rents that bought the expansive spreads of the 1920s, people were seeking modest but pleasantly efficient apartments at rents that were realistic within the strictures of a drastically-tightened economy. Chanin and Delemarre devised a complement of 52 different layouts for 416 apartments. They included one-bedroom units as duplexes or with terraces, and other features that previously could be found only in much larger apartments. Sensitive to the emotional trauma of trading down, the team realized that significantly spatial change would be more palatable if accompanied by a dramatic aesthetic one, so the building is pure Art Deco on both its façade and throughout its large U-shaped entrance lobby.

This limestone building shows a rich profusion of carved angels, heads, and fantastic beasts. It was designed in 1927 by architect John B. Peterkin.

The entire façade of this 1929 building was replaced in 1994 to remedy a persistent porosity that had been unsuccessfully treated in 1957 by the installation of full-height shiny aluminum cladding. The new brickwork restored the original Art Deco architectural design, which appears to have been a collaboration of architects George B. Post & Sons, Rosario Candela, and the project's developer Arthur Watkins Crisp. A 2011 project further improved the building by restoring the spectacular entrance doors and transom, which have been attributed on stylistic grounds to Edgar Brandt. This portal is a metallurgical mix of cast brass, bronze, and iron, plated with zinc, nickel, and cadmium. Builder Arthur Crisp (1881–1974) was a muralist, painter, and designer who bought several small buildings and razed them to erect this apartment house. He lost it to foreclosure in 1935. Then in 1945, its tenants bought the building for $500,000 and converted it to co-op ownership.

This Art Deco gem is a rarity on the Upper East Side, where classical architecture generally prevails. It was built in 1928 by Joseph Medill Patterson, publisher of *The New York Daily News*, to house his personal pied-à-terre in the penthouse. Lower full-floor apartments were taken by James A. Farley (later Postmaster General under Franklin Roosevelt) and his daughter Alicia, who founded *Newsday* in 1940. Architect Raymond Hood created vertical striping by alternating limestone piers with darker decorative metal spandrels, but later painting has obliterated the original effect. A neo-Mayan zig-zag frieze is complemented by elaborate metal panels on the entrance doors and simple flanking lanterns (all original).

The prior building on this site was the Tiffany house, a multiple dwelling of sorts, with separate quarters for Charles Tiffany (the Fifth Avenue jeweler) and the families of his children. The building remained as the residence of Louis Comfort Tiffany until his death in 1933. After buying the Tiffany site, investor John Thomas Smith hired Rosario Candela to plan a luxurious apartment house as a replacement for the old house. However, as Candela was known for the lavishly grand designs he had produced during the heady years of the 1920s, and as this was 1936 when the economic strictures of the Depression were still felt, he also retained architect Mott B. Schmidt, who was said by a Smith grandchild to have the task of keeping Candela within a tight budget. The total was $2.25 million, paid in cash by Smith for land and building. Originally there were 36 units that ranged from seven to 11 rooms apiece, including many duplexes. One of those was an extra-large apartment at the western half of the 14th and 15th floors that Smith retained for himself and his family. That one was altered in 1954 to form two duplexes, and other subdivisions and combinations have been made over the years. Original rents for the apartments ranged from $4,000 to $12,000 per year. The professional offices on the Madison Avenue side of the ground floor were constructed with additional long-span support beams to permit retail stores to use the space if necessary. Despite the significant rise in obtainable store rentals, the building's co-op board has not availed itself of this feature, and in any event it is not clear whether such an alteration to the façade would be permitted by the Landmarks Preservation Commission. The figural decoration surrounding the entrance was sculpted by Carl P. Jennewein, who was also responsible for some of the sculpture at Rockefeller Center.

This apartment house completed in 1930 has several Art Deco façade features, but the cast stone en-framement and central roundel of its entrance looks curiously predictive of the front of the Midtown (later Metro) Theater on Broadway near 100th Street, designed by apartment house architects Boak and Paris in 1933. Perhaps this is not surprising, as the architect of 49 East 96 Street was Thomas White Lamb (1871–1942), who was much better known for his theater designs. He was also responsible for the Pythian Temple at 135 West 70 Street, later converted to apartments.

Emery Roth was one of the four developers of the Normandy, in addition to serving as its architect (along with his two sons). Completed in 1939, the building is a hybrid of classical and Art Moderne design elements. Roth's aesthetic innovations at his apartment house at 888 Grand Concourse of two years earlier clearly guided the work on this building. Its site overlooked the then-recently-completed Riverside Park, which covered the unsightly and formerly exposed railroad tracks by the Hudson River. The most obvious similarity between 888 and 140 is seen at the entrances to the two apartment houses, fully evident despite the later signage covering the black granite cheek-walls at 888 and the filth on the mosaic tile flanking its entrance doors.

The brothers Blum, George (1870-1928) and Edward (1876-1944), were architects whose unusual aesthetic sense and extensive use of decorative terra-cotta yielded some of the most exceptional apartment houses in New York. Edward was the primary designer of the two, having received an architecture degree from Columbia University, with three years of graduate work at the École des Beaux Arts in Paris. Beginning in 1909, the brothers designed in rapid succession about seventy apartment buildings in styles that have variously been described as Art Nouveau, Arts and Crafts, Medieval Revival and Renaissance Revival, but which in reality have been unique to themselves. All have used brick of unusual colors and textures, glass mosaics, ceramic tiles, and inventive ironwork. But most of all they used highly textured decorative terra-cotta. They also designed about 60 commercial buildings of lesser visual interest. At the end of their career, they produced two buildings that also were ornamented in terra-cotta and were equally imaginative, but these two were reflective of the time and utilized brilliantly-colored glazed terra-cotta elements in strikingly Art Deco motifs. Working in both cases for the open-mindedly modern developers Albert and Charles Mayer, the Blums produced 210 East 68 Street (completed in 1928) and 235 East 22 Street (completed in 1930). This last one was on a very large plot that allowed for a private garden court separated from the sidewalk by an elaborate ironwork fence, and a narrow rear court connecting a secondary entrance to 23rd Street to the north.

III

210 East 68 Street

Completed in 1928 by architects George and Edward Blum for developers Albert and Charles Mayer, the bright orange brick and bold brightly-colored glazed terra-cotta ornamentation may have been used as a strategy to counteract the dreary atmosphere of the Third Avenue elevated train adjoining the building.

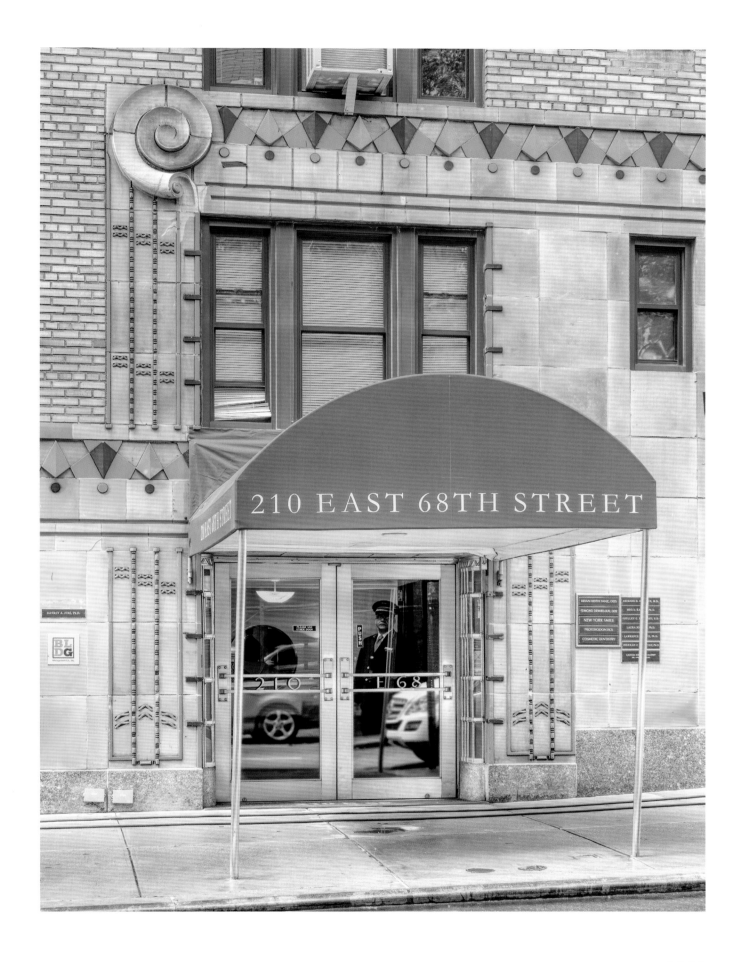

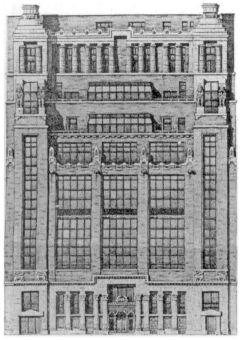

The theatricality of the building is logical as its original architect was Thomas W. Lamb, who was better known for his fantasy movie theaters. It was erected in 1927 for the Knights of Pythias, a fraternal organization, and included lodge rooms, a large auditorium, a bowling alley, a billiards room, and a gymnasium on the roof, all housed within a complex steel structure that is wrapped in a synthesis of Egyptian, Babylonian, and Assyrian themes rendered in brilliantly-polychromed glazed terra-cotta. After the Pythians departed in 1958 the building served as classrooms for the New York Institute of Technology and a studio for Decca Records where early Rock and Roll was recorded, along with the voices of Billie Holiday and Buddy Holly. Then in 1982 architect David Gura converted the building to residential usage by introducing windows in the original solid-masonry front façade and by carving the interior into duplex and simplex condominium units.

480 Park Avenue

At 19 stories, and extending 250 feet down East 58th Street, this is a very large building whose bulk doesn't begin to diminish until the setback terraces starting at the 14th floor. Completed in 1929 by Emery Roth for developer Sam Minskoff, the building exploited the provisions of the new Multiple-Dwelling law to provide those terraces for upper-floor tenants. Initially, amenities included a restaurant in the building that delivered, with hotel maid services if wanted. Apartments ranged from three rooms to fourteen, in simplex and duplex configurations. The building's aesthetic was Italian Renaissance revival, with elaborate terra-cotta ornamentation barely visible from the street. At floor 14 were angels above devils one floor below. The design scheme was evident at the avenue entrance and also at the side street doorway, no longer in active use.

The law under which this apartment hotel was built in 1926 considered it to be a commercial structure, thereby allowing it to be much taller than a conventional apartment house. It was designed by the architectural firms Sugarman & Berger and Helmle & Corbett working together. It is built of brick over a stone base. Its stone trim at the upper floors are augmented by pseudo-piers whose shadow lines are created by stacked darker brick. With expansive views of its low-rise Greenwich Village neighbors, there are duplex and terraced apartments at the many setbacks.

This is undoubtedly the most improbable apartment house in all of New York. It was built in 1929 by the charismatic Nicholas Roerich and was designed by skyscraper advocate Harvey Wiley Corbett with innovative corner windows where buildings normally have supporting steel columns. It originally incorporated a museum for the work of Roerich, a school, the Master Institute of United Arts, an auditorium for lectures and concerts, and rental apartments in the tower above that were supposed to support the entire operation. The timing was unfortunate, as the stock market crash shortly after the building opened caused its financial decline, and Roerich's influence declined with it. Tax-fraud accusations by the IRS against Roerich and a court-ordered receivership against the building led to predictable chaos. Roerich died in 1947, but the building continues as a cooperative apartment corporation.

This is certainly the grandest of any of the classic automobile entrances, but is wasn't the first. Half a century earlier the Dakota offered just such an amenity, but for carriages then. In 1906 The Langham on the next block north offered a cramped version of one, which was abandoned long ago. For River House of 1931, the luxury of delivery to the door by car was matched on the other side of the building by delivery by boat to its private floating dock, now sacrificed to a six-lane highway. The building was designed by architect William Bottomley for developer James Stewart. To resolve the problem of both 52nd and 53rd streets dead-ending at the river, he created the forecourt, and to overcome the 30-foot differential in the elevations of the two streets, there is also a seldom-used ramp that leads from the court down to 53rd street. This is truly a gated community excluding *hoi polloi*.

With this two-building complex, architect Robert A.M. Stern returned to the drive-in courtyard entrance last seen at River House. Working for the two Zeckendorf brothers, Stern emulated the appearance and luxury of what Rosario Candela had produced in the 1920s, but re-tuned to what apartment buyers of the 21st century require, or at least what the top one-tenth of one percent want. Stern pressed the developers repeatedly to spend more and more and to layer more and more luxury onto the project, an approach whose wisdom was proven when the prices for the units achieved record levels, and then resale prices went far higher. But the pedestrian entrance is low-key, simple, and reticent. The drive-in courtyard entry by its very nature is grander, but lest you miss the point, the stone moldings around the doorways repeat those of River House.

Designed by Pleasants Pennington and Albert Lewis and completed in October 1929 just when the stock market crashed, the building has simplex and duplex apartments of 8 to 13 rooms, with multiple bay windows enhancing the views out over the river, which is symbolized by the head of Neptune carved over the entrance. The site is a trapezoid that tapers down to accommodate only a single room at the south end.

Designed by John and Eliot Cross and completed in 1928, this was originally called the Yorkgate and was the first high-rise apartment house built on the avenue as redeveloped from its aged tenements and industrial buildings. With two expansive units per floor and a large penthouse with a long terrace on the river, this project of developers Henry Irons and A. Pearson Hoover clearly brought wealth to the neighborhood.

This contextual building is on a quiet little-traveled avenue a block away from the East River. Because of its distance from the subway and its minimal bus service, arrival by car influenced its design. The result devised by Robert A.M. Stern Architects in 2016 was to introduce a porte-cochère and motor court, accessed under a two-story archway on 80th Street that is reminiscent of those at the Belnord and the Apthorp on the other side of town. At the entrance for pedestrians on East End Avenue there is a shallow echo of that arched theme. The building picks up many of its details and its massing from the traditional apartment houses produced during the period between the two world wars. With the upper floors suggestive of those of 720 Park Avenue, there are bay windows, judiciously-placed balconettes, and multiple set-back terraces with stone balustrades. Carrying through the déja-vu approach, here and there are details taken from earlier Candela-designed apartment buildings. The market for these apartments, and thus the budget, was not sufficiently high to justify a full limestone façade, but the elegantly variegated gray-beige brick that instead was used makes a visually satisfying substitute.

521 Park Avenue was built in 1911 to designs of William A. Boring (1859–1937) that provided a single 13-room apartment on each floor. These were later subdivided to yield 27 units and in 1987 the building was converted to condominium ownership. In partnership with Edward L. Tilton (1861–1933), Boring designed the buildings on Ellis Island, for which his firm received the Gold Medal Award at the 1900 Paris Exposition. He also designed some sixty libraries and thirty theatres, as well as many private residences plus a comparable apartment house at 540 Park Avenue, since razed. In 1930 Boring joined the faculty at Columbia University and at the time of his death was Dean of its School of Architecture.

This was a condominium project of the Zeckendorf Development Company and the Whitehall Street Real Estate Fund (managed by Goldman Sachs & Company). It was erected in 2000 on the site of a 12-story apartment house of 1912 that had been built with two large apartments per floor but which in 1958 had been converted to office space. The architect for the new venture was Frank Williams, who died in 2010 at the age of 73. Williams had a 40-year practice that was thick with skyscrapers, which include the Trump Palace apartment house at 69th Street and Third Avenue, the residential portion of the World Wide Plaza at Ninth Avenue from 49th to 50th streets, and the Four Seasons Hotel on East 57th Street near Park Avenue, done in collaboration with Ioh Ming Pei. For 515 Park, Williams designed a 43-story tower that rises straight up on its east and south sides, but has set-backs and terraces on the north and west faces. In plan, there are two apartments per floor through the 14th floor. No sharing of elevator landings above that level, with the tower portion housing only six duplexes. Despite all that space, along with expansive views in all directions from the upper floors and elaborate amenities, the building was not well-received by the critics. It attempted to emulate the classic apartment houses of the 1920s by imitating their materials and details, but the scale was oversized, the materials often cheap, and the detailing heavy-handed. Robert A.M. Stern said it had an "awkward silhouette," and Paul Goldberger referred to the building as "particularly ungainly," adding that its façade is "a pretentious muddle."

123 *520 Park Avenue*

Unused air rights bought from the nearby church and the purchased right to cantilever over the adjacent Grolier Club allowed this exceptionally tall building to be developed on what seemed originally to be too small a site for a major structure. Then to pump up its importance it was given a Park Avenue address despite its being more than 150 feet from the Avenue. The result is a relatively small number of very grand apartments surrounded by richness and amenities.

DEVELOPER
ZECKENDORF DEVELOPMENT, LLC

ARCHITECTS
ROBERT A.M. STERN ARCHITECTS, LLP
SLCE ARCHITECTS, LLP

A.D. 2018

This 2018 apartment house designed by Robert A.M. Stern Architects brings the redeveloped Tribeca neighborhood down to the Hudson and reinforces the residential advantages of river's-edge living, restored only relatively recently after having been ignored for two centuries. Sheathed in an unusual pink French Beaumarière limestone with a two-story base of rusticated rough-chiseled masonry and classic detailing, the building resonates with the traditional apartment houses of the 1920s. This is particularly evident in the motor-court entry and its through-block driveway, a feature common to 10 Gracie Square.

A 1999 project of Robert A.M. Stern Architects, the building fits the aesthetic of its adjacent Tribeca neighborhood into the design constraints of the Battery Park City master plan, in whose north end it sits. But it also introduces the decidedly uptown element of a triple-arched covered-driveway entrance. The difference is that at One Sutton Place the porte-cochère is Italian Renaissance-inspired, and here it is reminiscent of the industrial architecture to the east of the building, reinforced by its paving material, the rough-hewn rectangular granite blocks colloquially called cobblestones, once ubiquitous within the area below Canal Street, and the bright red brick that is seen throughout the Tribeca area.

This 2014 project of the Brodsky Organization was designed by William Sofield as a condominium that reprises traditional apartment house elements in new ways. The canopy is structurally supported to be far more elegantly slim than the usual stretched canvas one, and the conventional evergreen trees in pots that flank most upscale New York City apartment houses here are rendered as two-story limestone carvings integral with the façade and backed by tall lancet windows. The entrance portal itself is enlarged to a very grand two-story arch that is fully glazed, yet the actual entry is only a single door, neatly bridging the gap between residential intimacy and civic importance. That prominence is reflected in the extension of the traditional limestone base to form an entry "tower" topped by an interpretation of a classical balustrade. Old is made new here.

67th Street Studio Buildings

Between 1903 and 1919, several grandly distinctive studio/apartment buildings were erected on West 67th Street between Columbus Avenue and Central Park West. The entire concept probably originated with Henry W. Ranger, an artist who was said (in his 1919 obituary in the *New York Times*) to have been irked by the need to pay $700 a year on a suitable painting studio in addition to spending $2000 a year for an appropriate apartment in which to live and to entertain patrons and friends. Ranger envisioned an apartment building in which double-height studios enjoying northern light would be included within living quarters of suitable size and beauty. Ranger's idea was adopted by another artist, Walter Russell, who has received most of the credit as he was the one who actually produced and promoted the projects. This goal was realized first in 27 West 67 Street in 1903, designed by Sturgis & Simonson, who also were responsible in 1905 for 15 West 67 Street. Simonson joined with George Mort Pollard in 1903 for 33 West 67 Street, and then Pollard alone designed the grandest of the lot at 1 West 67 Street, completed in 1919. The Hotel des Artistes was in fact an apartment-hotel as the building regulations barred a pure apartment house of the 150-foot height that the des Artistes reached. The original residents' dining room is now a grande-luxe public restaurant and the theater and the ballroom are now television studios, but the squash court and the swimming pool remain as amenities for the owners of what are now cooperative apartments. The building officially has only nine floors, but with its mezzanine levels it actually has twice that number. Originally there was a grandiose zig-zagged iron-and-glass marquee, which was replaced many years ago with a conventional but capacious canvas awning.

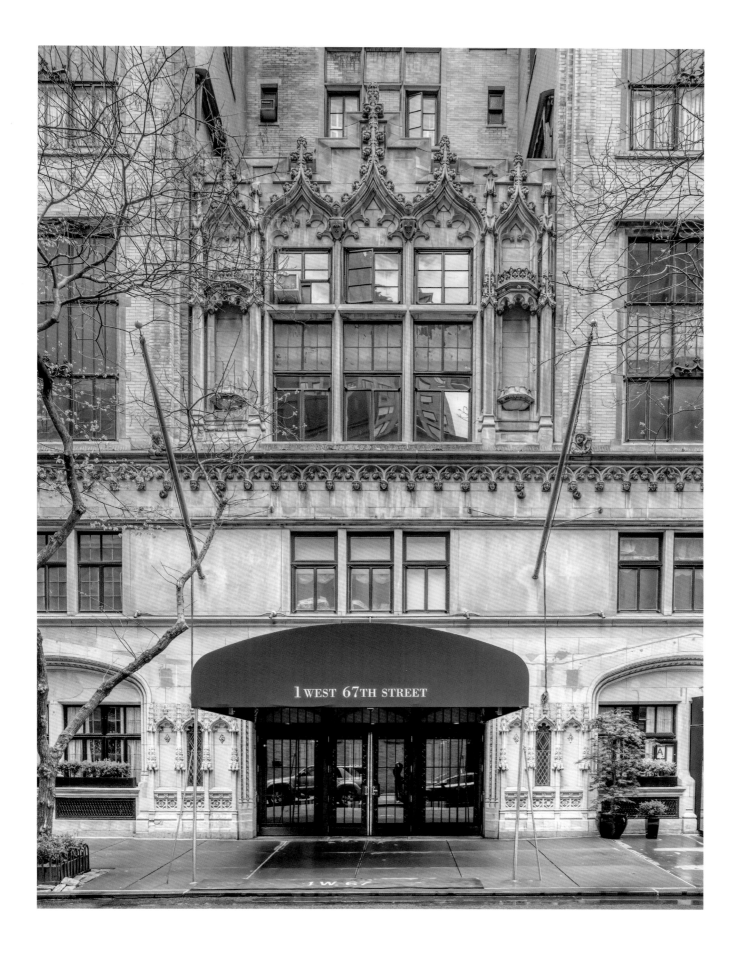

1 West 67 Street, Hotel des Artistes

27 West 67 Street, Sixty-Seventh Street Studio

266]

27 West 67 Street, Sixty Seventh Street Studio

15 West 67 Street, The Central Park Studios

15 West 67 Street, The Central Park Studios

33 West 67 Street

Discreet Doorways and Lesser Luminaries

32 St. Marks Place

Rome, Italy

246 East 4 Street

Architects of smaller apartment houses and less-imposing multiple dwellings are often just as interested in dressing up the entrances to their buildings as are those who design grander edifices. Here are several examples. The East 4th Street entry is an original neo-Gothic one that a zealous property manager glitzified with multiple paint colors and additional decorative castings. The others are more conventional and likely original to their buildings.

141 East 3 Street, Ageloff Towers

251 West 71 Street

126 East 12 Street

401 Eighth Avenue, Brooklyn, Roosevelt Arms

726 Ocean Avenue, Brooklyn

455 Ocean Avenue, Brooklyn

465 Ocean Avenue, Brooklyn

235 West End Avenue

393 West End Avenue

240 East 79 Street

325 East 79 Street

Disfigured Dignity

Brooklyn's Ocean Avenue has as much portal pretention as does Manhattan, but much of it has not fared well. Social and financial realities, along with insensitivity to architectural assets, have resulted in some sorry sights. The VALENCE at 716 Ocean Avenue boasted an especially pompous entrance enframement for a modest four-story semi-fireproof apartment house, but the crude removal of its cornice was gross vandalism. Security gates on entry arches, and anachronistic glass blocks and a steel door are painful to behold beneath splendid ornament.

716 Ocean Avenue, Brooklyn. VALENCE

446 Ocean Avenue, Brooklyn

540 Ocean Avenue, Brooklyn. CATHEDRAL ARMS

625 Ocean Avenue, Brooklyn. ARISTA

666 Ocean Avenue, Brooklyn. CAMEO COURT

[277

KENNETH GRANT is an architectural photographer with a special passion for the buildings of his native New York. Originally a journalist and web producer, he now records the buildings around him in New York, showing the results at www. newyorkitecture.com where he provides images and histories of significant buildings and neighborhoods, including those of Philadelphia, Washington DC, Richmond, Cincinnati, and other cities.

ANDREW ALPERN is an architectural historian, architect, and attorney who is an expert on historic apartment houses in New York. He has ten prior books, six of which tell the stories of some of New York's architectural assets and the people behind them. Alpern has also published scores of articles about historical architecture and particular buildings. He donated to the Columbia University Libraries his 50-year archive of the work of writer/artist Edward Gorey, and his 50-year collection of 300 years of architectural drawing instruments, which have been made obsolete by computer drafting. He has been a resident of Manhattan since 1938.

SIMON FIELDHOUSE is an Australian artist who was struck by the elegance of the entrances to so many of New York's apartment buildings when he first visited the city. He has also painted historic buildings of England, Italy and Australia. He has had solo exhibitions throughout Australia and presents his work through his website at www.simonfieldhouse.com.

INDEX

SET IN

BODONI AND BICKHAM TYPES.

DESIGN AND TYPOGRAPHY BY

JERRY KELLY.